A Hundred Years at St Bride's

Kinnear House in Charlotte Street. Where it all began, in 1895.

A Hundred Years at St Bride's

The History of St Bride's and Lomond Schools,
with many Larchfield photographs.

Dr Martin Everett

ISBN 0 954507002

Published by
Lomond School
01436 672476

Printed by
Cordfall Ltd
G21 2QA

This book is dedicated to the late Mrs Irene Giles,
Secretary at Lomond School, 1989–2001.
A friend to all at Lomond.
And:
To all pupils and members of staff, teaching and non-teaching,
who have been a part of Helensburgh High School, St Bride's,
Larchfield and Lomond Schools during the last 158 years,
especially those who are not mentioned individually in the following pages.

Contents

Introduction

As I ran onto the train
My heart pounded with
Anticipation . . .
My eyes roared like flames
Before the tears dissolved
The ashes.

(Keith Gilmore)

The poem above, which was written by a pupil who was in S.1 at the time of the St Bride's fire, illustrates the difference between a child's fantasy and the awful reality that greeted staff and pupils on the morning of 27 February 1997. A school is much more than a building, and yet—children, teachers and headteachers come and go, whilst the building spans the generations and provides a fixed point of reference. Ardenlee, the private house which became St Bride's School, was built in 1859, and stood for 138 years. For 95 years it was the home of St Bride's and Lomond Schools; the fire destroyed it in a few hours.

If indeed the cause of the fire was arson, as was strongly suspected, then the unifying effect of their deed is probably beyond the comprehension of the perpetrators. The outpouring of affection, love and support from pupils, staff, parents, former pupils and local people was truly overwhelming, and gave everyone involved in running the School the impetus to carry on throughout all the resultant difficulties and at the same time to plan a new and better school for the twenty-first century.

So, most of the old school, and all of the original Ardenlee, with the exception of its former coach house, is gone, and with it the scene of the memories of thousands of former pupils and hundreds of former teachers. I hope that this book will help to preserve some of those memories. As well as being the history of a school (or in fact four schools), the book is also a social history, and it is interesting to see that whilst there have of course been many changes within the School and within society in general over the last hundred years, many of the aspects of St Bride's that were dear to the heart of Miss Renton, the School's first Headmistress, have stood the test of time.

The year 2002 marked the 25th Anniversary of the formation of Lomond School, and also the 100th Anniversary of the establishment of St Bride's School on the present site, so it is perhaps appropriate to pause and look back at over 140 years of Helensburgh history. Having done so, however, let us, as the Lomond motto *Prospiciamus* suggests, look forward.

M. Everett, 2003

(Dr Martin Everett has been Head of English at Lomond School since 1984.)

Part One:

1895–1929. The Miss Renton Years

The Girls' School Company

At the start of the new Millennium, the idea of equal opportunities for girls is so deeply engrained in our society that it is enshrined in law. But equality of the sexes, however much it may be taken for granted by the present generation of Lomond's female pupils, is a fairly recent phenomenon, and the fact that St Bride's School came into existence at all is due to the far-sightedness and idealism of a group of professional, academic and business men who wanted the same quality of education for their daughters that their sons already received at Britain's best Public (i.e. fee-paying) schools.

The Girls' School Company was thus founded in Glasgow in 1879 with the aim of establishing in the city a Public School for girls that would rival similar prestigious Schools for boys such as Eton and Winchester south of the border. The Company was governed by a board of thirteen 'Directors', all of whom were male, and it was technically a commercial company. The first Chairman was Mr J.L.K. Jamieson, engineer and shipbuilder, who was succeeded upon his death shortly afterwards (1883) by the Rev. Professor Thomas Lindsay of Glasgow United Free College, who served until 1914.

The Directors' aims were remarkably enlightened for the times, and it could be argued that they are still applicable to Lomond over 120 years later. They intended that the School should '. . . enjoy a degree of liberty and elasticity in regard to methods and curricula' which at that time did not exist in the newly-established state schools, and which was beyond the resources of the host of small private schools that existed in middle-class areas. Girls were to have '. . .

Miss Renton in her retirement year, 1929.

11

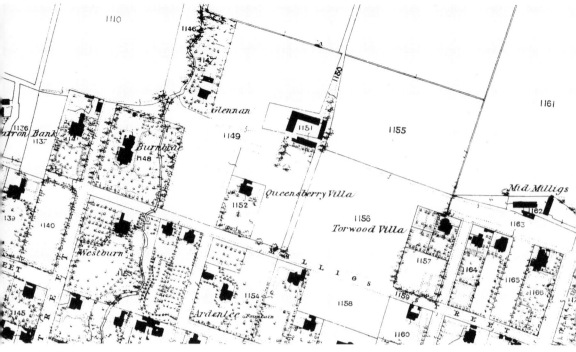

Section of 1864 Ordnance Survey map of Helensburgh.

Ardenlee (1154) and Burnbrae (1148) can be discerned. Note the separate coach-house belonging to Ardenlee which is now the only surviving part of the original building—the 2003 Music Studio. A fountain is shown in the grounds, on the site of what became St Bride's tennis court; this area is now occupied by the new Larchfield Hall, the dining-hall and sixth-year centre. There also seems to be a walled garden or orchard behind the coach-house; this area is now the site of the gymnasium. Ashmount and Clarendon (1156) (Torwood Villa) have yet to be built.

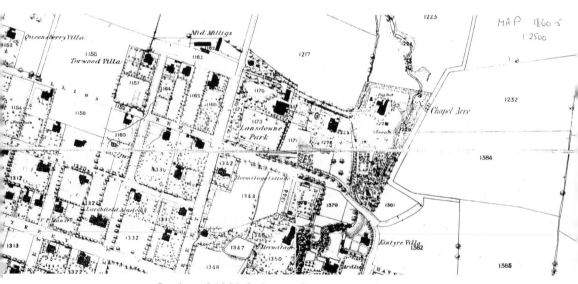

Section of 1864 Ordnance Survey map of Helensburgh.

Larchfield Academy (1321), Lansdowne Park (1173) and the site of Kintyre Villa (1382) at the junction of Charlotte Street and Havelock Street can be discerned. Kintyre Villa was purchased by the Girls' School Company in 1895 and renamed Kinnear House. It was the home of Helensburgh High School for Girls until 1902.

a sound and liberal education which should make for the development of individuality and a sense of responsibility'.

The first School established by the Company was The Park, in Glasgow's city-centre. It opened in 1880 under the Headship of Miss Georgina Kinnear. 'The High School for Girls' in Helensburgh followed in 1895, and St Columba's, Kilmacolm, in 1897. The first Headmistress of Helensburgh High School, and later of St Bride's, Miss J.B.M. Renton, was thus accurately able to describe St Bride's as '. . . the daughter of The Park School'.

Helensburgh High School and Private Education in the Town

The distinction made by the Directors in their plans for the Company's schools between Public schools and private schools, both of which were fee-paying, was an important one. The Education Act (Scotland) of 1872 led to the formation of School Boards across the country; specifically, in Helensburgh, the Parish of Row (Rhu) School Board, which established Hermitage School in 1880 on land belonging to the Cramb family's Hermitage House, to be followed by James Street Infants and Primary School (1890), and Clyde Street School (1904). The James Street School subsequently became St Joseph's Primary School (1933); it was demolished in 1980, and sheltered housing, (Waverley Court), now occupies the site. Before the 1872 Act, Helensburgh's only parish school was the quaintly-named 'Ragged Industrial School' in Grant Street, built in 1853 on the site of the present gas-works, which came under the control of the Row School Board at the time of the Act. It was demolished in 1876 when the gas-works was built. There were also two church schools: the West Free Church School in Colquhoun Street, and The Established Church School in East Clyde Street. However, both before the 1872 Act, which made education compulsory for all children between the ages of 5 and 13, and after it, there were numerous small private schools in Helensburgh, the first recorded dating back to 1807.

The opening of the Helensburgh–Glasgow railway line in 1857 led to the rapid expansion of the town, in particular the west end where before the 1997 fire, five properties belonging to Lomond: St Bride's (Stafford Street); Burnbrae (Campbell Street), Ashmount and Clarendon (Millig Street), and Larchfield (West Montrose Street), were situated. This expansion was so rapid that between the census of 1851 and that of 1861, the town's population increased by 65 per cent. One result of the rapid development of the streets of prosperous stone villas and the large Victorian families which they housed was a major increase in the demand for private education. In the 1860s there were two private schools in West Clyde Street, and another in West Montrose Street, whilst by 1875, Ashmount, Barwood in Montrose Street; Glenfruin House and Springfield Academy in James Street; Larchfield, and Kintyre Villa at 25 Charlotte Street were all operating as private schools. By 1883 Ardenlee in Stafford Street, Dunclutha in George Street and Springbank in James Street had been added to the list, to be followed by Brownhill and Thornden in Colquhoun Street by 1890. The latter establishment (at number 64) was run by Mr and Mrs Porteous, who later took over Ardenlee, which became St Bride's.

In 1895, Miss Nicol's 'Ladies' Boarding School' at Kintyre Villa in Charlotte Street,

Kinnear House c.1913.
Supervised by Miss Renton, it became the senior girls' boarding-house for St Bride's in 1902.

which she had run for well over twenty years, was purchased by the Girls' School Company, and on 2 September it opened as Helensburgh High School for Girls. The house, which still stands by the grass triangle in Charlotte Street at the junction with Victoria Road, was built as a private residence c.1866, and was named Kintyre Villa. However, the Company renamed it Kinnear House in honour of the Headmistress of The Park School. This name can still be seen on the gate-post today. Miss J. B. M. Renton, who had taught in Manchester and also under Miss Kinnear at The Park, was appointed Headmistress at the age of 31. She was to hold this position for 34 years.

The school opened, after some refurbishment, with 40 pupils inherited from Miss Nicol, but by the end of the session this number had grown to 59, swelled by several pupils of The Park who lived in Helensburgh, including a future St Bride's Head Girl, E. Mary Oastler, who on her arrival at Kinnear House was amazed to find that the school had green desks and did not use slates. According to *The Helensburgh and Gareloch Times* the Directors were also very proud of the fact that '. . . every scholar has her own chair and desk', and of the 'entirely new system of drainage' that had been installed. Indeed, the renovations, which had occupied the summer holidays, had produced a 'complete transformation' in the School, which boasted '. . . large, airy, well-ventilated classrooms', the decoration of which was 'in excellent taste'. Helensburgh High School would rank, the Directors claimed, as '. . . one of the best-equipped establishments . . . in Scotland', and would meet a 'felt want' in the town.

ARDENLEE SCHOOL,

FOR THE BOARD AND

EDUCATION OF YOUNG LADIES

AND

PREPARATORY SCHOOL FOR BOYS.

———

PRINCIPALS : MR AND MRS PORTEOUS

(Of Twenty-five Years' Practical Experience in Tuition).

———

YOUNG LADIES are taught all the Branches and Accomplishments requisite in a liberal course of FEMALE EDUCATION by thoroughly experienced Masters. Special advantages for Higher English, Modern Languages, Music, Singing, Drawing, Painting, and Drill. Successful preparation for University and Musical Examinations.

Boys receive a thorough grounding in all the Essential Branches of a PRACTICAL MODERN EDUCATION. Preparation for Civil Service Examinations, Scholarships, Public Schools, Commercial Life, or University.

The Teaching, from long experience, is of a high order of efficiency. Each Boy receives special care and individual attention, so conducive to success in all Examinations.

MUSIC DEPARTMENT.

A Resident German Master, of the highest eminence in every branch of Musical Education, is kept exclusively for this School ; also, a Resident Foreign Governess, trained in a German Conservatoire, devotes special attention to this Department.

MODERN LANGUAGES.

Special facilities are offered for acquiring FRENCH and GERMAN. Mrs PORTEOUS, having been educated in France and Germany, knows the grammar and literature of both languages thoroughly, and speaks them fluently, and, together with the assistance of a Resident German Master and French Governess, gives particular attention to this department. *Every Pupil in French or German will receive a Lesson Daily.*

PRIVATE LESSONS for Advanced Pupils in French or German, or those preparing for Examinations in Pianoforte, Harmonium, Violin, and Singing, apart from School, can be arranged at suitable hours.

DRAWING and PAINTING, ELOCUTION, DANCING, and SHORTHAND are taught by Specialists.

BOARD.

There is Extensive and Very Superior Accommodation for Boarders, who are under the careful supervision of Mrs PORTEOUS and Resident Governess.

The greatest pains is taken to insure the domestic comfort and physical well-being of the Pupils.

Refined and comfortable Home, cheerful, well-ventilated Rooms, perfect Sanitary arrangements. The Principals can refer to Parents and Former Pupils in every quarter of the globe.

Permanent Home for Anglo-Indians.

HOURS.

The School Hours are from 9 A.M. to 3.30 P.M. The Younger Pupils from 10 A.M., and leave at 12.30. Seniors get from 1 to 2 o'clock for dinner or lunch. Day Pupils can dine with the Boarders at 1 o'clock.

———

TERMS MODERATE AND INCLUSIVE.

———

NEXT SESSION BEGINS SEPT. 2ND.

———

Prospectus, with view of Premises and Terms, on application, or at MACNEUR & BRYDEN'S.

THE

GIRLS' SCHOOL CO., LTD.

———

HIGH SCHOOLS FOR GIRLS.

———

LYNEDOCH STREET, GLASGOW, AND CHARLOTTE ST., HELENSBURGH.

———

President :

SIR CHARLES TENNANT, Bart., of The Glen.

Chairman :

Rev. PROF. LINDSAY, D.D., Free Church College.

Directors :

J. M. Cunningham, 3 Crown Circus.
Rev. James Dodds, D.D., Manse, Corstorphine.
A. A. Ferguson, 11 Grosvenor Terrace.
Professor Jack, LL.D., The University.
Robert Murdoch, 7 Park Street, East.
John E. Watson, 16 Belhaven Terrace.
J. B. Wingate, 9 Crown Terrace.
Professor Young, M.D., The University.
John A. Spens, 169 West George Street.
Robert Laidlaw, 6 Marlborough Terrace.
A. M. Lindsay, Esq., 1 Park Gate.

Secretary and Treasurer :

D. HILL JACK, 194 St. Vincent Street, Glasgow.

———

CHARLOTTE STREET, Helensburgh.

HEAD MISTRESS—MISS RENTON.

Assistant Mistresses :

Miss SAMUEL, Miss C. T. RENTON, Miss WHITLING, Miss LINDSAY, Miss MACDONALD, Miss WAUGH, and Mistresses for Music and Dancing.

This School will be opened for the first time on THURSDAY, 5th September. The Head Mistress will attend daily at the School to enrol Pupils, from TUESDAY, 3rd September.

All Books and Stationery used in the School will be furnished to the Pupils free of charge. Little Boys will be admitted to the Initiatory Department.

The Course of Study, both in the Lower and Upper Departments, will be the same as in the Company's School in Glasgow, Chemistry excepted.

Music, Painting, and Dancing are taught as extra Subjects.

Pupils who wish to dine at the School in the middle of the day can do so at a moderate charge.

———

Prospectuses can be obtained of MACNEUR & BRYDEN'S.

August 1895.

Advertisements from the *Helensburgh and Gareloch Times* for Ardenlee and for the opening of Helensburgh High School for Girls in Charlotte Street. Ardenlee, which became St Bride's in 1902, after its purchase by the Girls' School Company, offered boarding accommodation, perhaps upstairs in what were the Maths classrooms at the time of the 1997 fire. It also provided a 'permanent home for Anglo-Indians', as these children could be reunited with their parents only by ship.

Helensburgh High School, whose staff, according to the local paper, were 'carefully selected' and of 'the highest class', having '. . . elsewhere earned for themselves a high reputation . . .', aimed to correct defects in girls' education nationally, highlighted in the recent *Report* of the Schools' Inquiry Commission. This had pinpointed a general '. . . want of thoroughness and formulation, want of system . . .' and 'slovenliness . . . showy superficiality, inattention to rudiments . . .' with 'undue time given to accomplishments, and these not taught in any satisfactory or organised manner'. It apparently quickly succeeded in achieving these aims, for when it was inspected in 1897, (Lomond was to undergo a similar inspection, with broadly similar results, nearly 100 years later), the School was complimented on the 'rapid progress' made since its inception, and according to the *Helensburgh and Gareloch Times*, the inspectors had commented that the School 'promised a career of ever-extending usefulness'. Indeed, under Miss Renton, the High School was conducted with 'rare professional skill', and had an 'excellent tone'. Pupils were complimented on their 'refined manners' and their 'clear and cultured pronunciation', whilst the inspectors were particularly pleased with the lessons in practical geometry 'nothing could be better', and the 'fine pronunciation' of the French mistress, (which was perhaps unsurprising, as the lady in question, Mlle Humbert, was a Swiss native speaker of French!). At the Prize-Giving of 1898, (reported in the local paper), however, Miss Renton was not afraid to be critical, commenting on the girls' lack of natural aptitude for languages, in particular. She confessed herself to be disappointed in the progress of many of her pupils, particularly the older girls, despite the advantages of small classes and the consequent individual attention. (Interestingly, the Rev. Prof. Lindsay, Chairman of the Company, argued at the same Prize-Giving for larger classes, which he felt produced 'inspiration, spirit and enthusiasm'. He also stated that in his view the bicycle was 'the greatest gift given to the women of the nineteenth century'.) Miss Renton went on to stress the importance of Latin in helping to remedy the 'arrears of spelling and grammar' which she felt her pupils possessed. The problem was to remedy these whilst still finding time to 'cultivate taste for the beauties of the language', a problem which perhaps still faces teachers of English today.

By 1898, the School roll had reached 84, and, in keeping with their long-term aims of establishing a 'high-class boarding school', in 1899 the Directors established Miss Renton and ten girls in two adjoining ground-floor flats in Prince Albert Terrace. In the same year, two local parents, Mr W. Anderson, of Inistore, (now Glenkin) in John Street and Dr Sewell, of Rosemount (Argyle Street) were elected to the Glasgow Board of Directors, and they were soon followed by a third, the artist Mr R.G. Paterson. In these early days of the High School, games were played on the front lawn of Kinnear House which in 2003 forms part of the grounds of Parklands School. Hockey was played with walking-sticks and balls of netted string. The field near the curling-pond in Havelock Street was also used, the girls being required to wear their red peaked caps for games. (The caps bore a Latin motto, meaning 'In God's hands we shall walk with feeling'.) The first official sporting fixture took place in 1900, when a hockey match was played against St Columba's.

By the time of the 1901 Prize-giving, which was again held in July in the Victoria Halls' Pillar Hall, Miss Renton was able to report increased enrolments in the lower school,

EDUCATION.

LARCHFIELD ACADEMY.

PUPILS will be Enrolled on WEDNESDAY Morning, 4th September, at Ten o'clock, and the regular work of the Classes will Begin at Nine o'clock on THURSDAY, the 5th. New Books should not be bought before the Opening Day, on and after which the Books for the First Quarter will be in Messrs MACNEUR & BRYDEN'S. 5th August, 1895.

ASHMOUNT.

MISSES MURDOCH will Re-Open their School on WEDNESDAY, 4th September, at Ten o'clock.

Advanced Classes for English Literature, for the Study of the French and German Languages, and the Literature of those languages, with conversation, will be continued.

Misses MURDOCH will be assisted by the following Teachers :—

Mr GEORGE P. PAULIN, M.A. ; Mr ARTHUR F. PRICE (Cantab.); Mr VALLANCE, Mr PHILLIPS, Mr BROWN, Mr HELMORE, Mademoiselle MADELHOFFER, Miss GILLIES, Mrs ST. CLAIR BLACK and Assistants.

Prospectuses at MACNEUR & BRYDEN'S.

THE

Girls' School Company,

INCORPORATED IN THE YEAR 1877.

President:
SIR CHARLES TENNANT, BART., OF THE GLEN.

Chairman :
REV. PROFESSOR LINDSAY, D.D., FREE CHURCH COLLEGE.

Directors:

J. M. CUNNINGHAM, J.P., Helensburgh.	Prof. YOUNG, M.D., The University, Glas'w
A. A. FERGUSSON, 11 Grosvenor Terrace, Glasgow.	J. A. SPENS, 169 West George St., Glasgow
Prof. JACK, LL.D., The University, Glas'w	R. LAIDLAW, 6 Marlborough Terrace, ,,
R. MURDOCH, 7 Park Circus Place, ,,	A. M. LINDSAY, M.A., 1 Park Gate, ,,
FRED. L. M. MOIR, Barclaven, Kilmalcolm.	WM. ANDERSON, Inistore, Helensburgh.
DAVID TODD, Greyneuk, Kilmalcolm.	W. R. SEWELL, M.D., Rosemount, ,,
	J. E. WATSON, 16 Belhaven Terrace, Gla'ow

Secretary :
D. HILL JACK, 141 WEST GEORGE STREET, GLASGOW.

The High School for Girls,
CHARLOTTE STREET, HELENSBURGH.

Head=Mistress. = = = = = **Miss Renton.**

The Staff consists of Certificated and Trained Mistresses.

COURSE OF STUDY.

The Curriculum includes—Scripture and the usual English Subjects, Arithmetic and Mathematics, Natural Science, French, German or Latin, Drawing, Class Singing, Swedish Drill, and Sewing.

There are Three Sections in the School—Preparatory (including Kindergarten Class), Lower, and Upper.

BOYS ARE ADMITTED TO THE PREPARATORY SCHOOL.

MUSIC, PAINTING, and DANCING ARE EXTRA SUBJECTS.

EXAMINATIONS.

The School is annually inspected by independent Examiners. In Form VI. Girls may prepare for University Entrance Examinations.

BOARDERS.

Boarding-House is under the personal direction of the Head Mistress. Special terms and arrangements for Weekly Boarders.

Prospectus on application to the Head-Mistress, the Secretary, or Macneur & Bryden, Helensburgh.

Opposite: **Staff and Upper School pupils outside Kinnear House, 1899.**
Back row:
Mlle Humbert,
Miss de Veule,
Marjorie Hughes,
Mimi Gilmour,
Miss Whitling,
Miss C Renton,
Miss Lindsay,
Emily MacPherson,
Mabel Lamont,
Grace Bryden,
Edith Suckling,
Daisy MacKay,
Madge Lunan,
Miss Renton
(Headmistress).
Front row:
Chrissie MacPherson,
Minnie Leitch,
Alice Lunan,
May Garvie,
Agnes Buchanan,
Kitty Lunan,
Mary Roberts,
Eliza White,
Jean MacPherson,
Joan Hughes,
Muriel Whitling.

which she attributed to the School's emphasis on English and mathematics. Session 1900–1901 '. . . held the best promise for the future of any year . . . yet'. Miss Renton was also looking ahead to the proposed purchase of a larger building, Ardenlee in Stafford Street, which would be 'more central and accessible', and thus would further improve the enrolment of young children, for whom, in the days before cars were to be seen in Helensburgh, (horse-drawn sledges were still in use during snowy winters), there was a problem in physically getting to school. The Headmistress also devoted much of her report to the need for games, which were perhaps thought by some people to be 'unladylike'. Miss Renton, however, felt that:

> . . . by means of games, girls develop qualities which make them later capable women in their own homes, or useful members of the community . . . learning quickness of thought and action, fairness, judgement, and . . . especially unselfishness.

She stressed, however, that hockey was the only organised game played at the School, and that exercise was '. . . always in moderation and under supervision.' Moreover, there was 'an absolute check upon roughness'.

1901 also saw the foundation of the Former Pupils' Guild, which was to play such an important part in the life of the School for nearly 70 years, and which still exists today in the form of the Lomond Society. Miss Renton presided over the Guild's first meeting, which was held in Helensburgh High School on the evening of 26 November. Eleven former pupils, eight staff and two former members of staff attended. The evening's programme consisted of music and dancing, and there was an exhibition of the girls' holiday photography and other holiday work, which would doubtless have included embroidery. Regrettably, according to the Guild's *Minute-Book*, '. . . there were only two collections of wild flowers'.

Opposite: **'Middle School' of Helensburgh High School, outside Kinnear House, 1899, with Miss Renton, back row, far right.**

Ardenlee and Alexander Nisbet Paterson

The expanding roll already referred to, and the desire for a more central location, had led the Directors to search for a new building. Ardenlee, in Stafford Street was purchased from James Wilkins for the sum of £2,000. Ardenlee had been built as a private house in

1859, and its grounds comprised what had originally been two plots. The smaller of the two plots had been purchased by Thomas Buchanan, a joiner, from Sir James Colquhoun in 1856, but had not been developed. Thomas Watson, a lawyer and writer, bought the land from Buchanan in 1858, and the following year he purchased the adjoining plot from Sir James. The annual feu duty to be paid on the combined plot was £31 10/-, (£31 50p). Interestingly, Sir James Colquhoun retained all mining and quarrying rights on the land, whilst Watson was responsible for laying out and maintaining footpaths around the plot, sewers and half the width of the bordering roads, (Stafford Street, Millig Street and John Street). The deeds allowed for the construction of a house of a 'neat and tasteful design', built in a 'substantial manner'. The value of the property erected was to exceed £1,000, and a wall not exceeding 7'6" in height was to be erected along the Millig Street side, and

Ardenlee School,

BOARDING AND DAY SCHOOL FOR BOYS.

Principal, = Mr James Porteous.

The Course of Study embraces English, French, German, Latin, Arithmetic, Mathematics, Science, Writing, Book-keeping, Short-hand, Drawing, Pianoforte-Music, Singing, Drill, and Dancing.

Courses of Lectures are given during the Session on subjects likely to interest and instruct the Pupils.

Religious Instruction is given in all the Classes.

Thorough instruction in all the essential branches of a liberal education is provided, and the greatest attention is paid to the more Advanced Branches.

Special arrangements are made for Boys requiring Special Training for Business, the University, Public Schools, or Civil Service.

French and German are Taught by Resident Natives.

Music (Pianoforte, Violin, Singing), Drawing and Painting, Science, Elocution, Drill, and Shorthand are taught by Specialists.

Extensive Grounds for Recreation.

The Premises are extensive and conveniently situated, and have been specially adapted for Scholastic purposes.

Sanitary and other appliances are of the most approved description.

PERMANENT HOME for ANGLO-INDIANS.

TERMS MODERATE AND INCLUSIVE.

NEXT SESSION BEGINS 1st SEPTEMBER.

Prospectus containing full particulars on application.

Advertisement from the *Helensburgh and Gareloch Times*, late 1890s.

When Mr James Porteous rented Ardenlee School from Mr James Wilkins in the early 1890s, it was a school for boys only. However, by the time that the Girls' School Company purchased the building from Wilkins in 1901, Porteous and his wife were running a school for 'young ladies' whilst boys' education was provided at Preparatory level only. Perhaps competition from the nearby Larchfield had proved too severe. (See also p.15.)

for 50 feet along John Street. (This was presumably the stone wall, which still stands today.) The address of the property was then 62 John Street, probably because Stafford Street had not been fully developed. The plan of the property taken from an Ordnance Survey map of 1860, shows Ardenlee with its coach-house (the 2003 Studio, now part of Lomond's Music Department), a walled garden where the gymnasium now stands, and a fountain at the bottom end of what became the St Bride's tennis court; this is where the new dining-hall (Larchfield Hall) now stands. The long driveway sweeping round to the coach-house can also be clearly seen, and this does not seem to have changed in layout until the 1997 fire and the subsequent construction of the new building. Indeed, the contours of the present car-park still follow the lines of the old drive. (In 1869, Watson's coachman was David Black.)

In 1875, Ardenlee was purchased by James Wilkins, of Bournemouth, who converted it into a boys' school. The house was extended in 1880. Wilkins ran the School himself until at least 1891, but by the time of its acquisition by the Girls' School Company, it was being rented from him by Mr and Mrs James Porteous, who had previously run Thornden School at 54 Colquhoun Street, and was known as

Ardenlee School for Young Ladies and Little Boys. (Wilkins was by this time living in Cheltenham.) Thus between 1891 and 1901, Porteous changed Ardenlee from a boys' to a girls' school.

To purchase and expand Ardenlee, £3,000 was raised by share subscription. One contributor was The Right Honourable A. Bonar Law, M.P., reputedly the owner of the town's first motor-car, who lived at Kintillo in Stafford Street, and who in October 1922 became Prime Minister for a short time before dying of throat cancer in 1923. Bonar Law presented Miss Renton with a silver cigarette case as a token of thanks when his daughter left the School; unfortunately, the Headmistress was a non-smoker! He was also Chancellor of the Exchequer during World War I, and lost his two sons in the conflict. In 1901, before the School moved from Kinnear House, Alexander Nisbet Paterson, architect, who had at least one daughter (Viola) at the School, designed various alterations and additions to Ardenlee, including the present St Bride's School Hall, built into the back of the house, which survived the 1997 fire. The reconstructed building, renamed St Bride's, was formally opened on 13 October 1902. Kinnear House became the new School's boarding-house.

Interestingly, other parts of St Bride's that were designed by Paterson also survived the fire. In 1908 he designed the corridors and laboratory (Mr Allen's Geography room until 1998; now Mr I. Macdonald's Music room in 2002), that linked the main building to the coach-house, (the Studio), which by then was St Bride's gymnasium. In 1923 he also designed the East Wing, and in particular the Bridesian Library. The care that he took with the furnishing and decoration of the Bridesian is obvious from the lengthy letters, which still survive, that he wrote to the then President of the Bridesian Guild, Miss Eileen Swinburne.

Paterson had trained at the Ecole des Beaux Arts in Paris in 1896, and moved to Helensburgh in 1897. He designed a number of prominent local landmarks, including the extension to the Municipal Buildings, (complete with cat); the War Memorial in Hermitage Park and the chancel of the now-demolished St Bride's Church. He was also responsible for the interiors of St Columba's Church and the Victoria Halls. Additionally, he designed a number of houses in Helensburgh, including several in Millig Street, (e.g. The Turret and Drum Millig), and his own house, Longcroft, (1901) in West Rossdu Drive. Further afield, he designed a large number of projects in Glasgow, including the National Bank buildings in St Enoch's Square, and the Eye Infirmary in Charlotte Street. Paterson was also a painter, and exhibited at the Royal Academy.

Saint Bride

The School's new name was chosen with great care. It had local associations, since according to legend it was thought that the ancient chapel, which once stood at Kirkmichael, Garelochhead, was associated with St Bride, as was the chapel in Glen Fruin at Kilbride, (meaning 'the church of Bride'). Saint Bride, (Brigid or Bride of Kildare) is one of the three principal Irish saints; the church in London's famous Fleet Street is named after her, and in Scotland, churches have been founded in her honour from Douglas in Lanarkshire to

The sitting-room at Kinnear House in 1913, when it was the Senior Girls' boarding-house.

The grounds of Kinnear House, now the site of Parklands School.

Lewis in the Outer Hebrides. According to legend, St Bride came to Scotland from Ireland and established a church at Abernethy; in 1460, Abernethy was created a collegiate church, the seal of which is preserved in the British Museum. A copy of this seal was lent to the School on its foundation by the then Minister of Abernethy, and one side of the seal formed the St Bride's School badge. It still forms half of Lomond's badge today. St Bride is shown with nimbus (aura, or halo), holding a crozier in her right hand. All the elements of the badge are symbolic: the lamp being held by the Saint represents the light of knowledge; the fire stands for hospitality, and the milking-pail represents practicality. According to legend, St Bride sheltered the baby Jesus under a rowan tree, covering Him with seaweed to hide Him from Herod. The oyster-catchers which are depicted also helped to protect the baby, whilst the dandelions are known as 'St Bride's flowers'. The background landscape is intended to be Clydeside's hills and lochs. These details can be clearly seen in the beautiful plaque in the Bridesian Library, designed by Miss Evelyn Beale, although for reasons of space most are omitted from the half of Lomond's badge that depicts St Bride today.

On the School's occupation of Ardenlee, and the change of the building's and the School's name, an oval badge showing St Bride with a cow was substituted for the HHS (Helensburgh High School) monogram in black, red and gold which had adorned the girls' hats, although at this stage, the School colours remained the same. It appears that in the first days of Helensburgh High School, the only signs of a uniform were blue and white ribbons attached to straw boaters (presumably in summer only), but the colours were soon changed to scarlet and black. After a few years, most of the girls wore red blouses, and a blue tie with black or navy gym-tunics, the hems of which could be no more than 4 inches from the ground. The monogram, and then the St Bride's badge, was worn on the girls' hats to distinguish them from the pupils of Hermitage School, who also wore red and black or red and navy blue. For this reason the School colours were changed to dark green tunics with light green blouses in 1911.

The First Years of the Guild and St Bride's

In the last year or so at Helensburgh High School, the Guild continued to hold regular social, literary and musical meetings. It also ran holiday competitions for the girls. In February 1902, the Guild hosted a lecture on 'The Greek Drama', complete with 'magic lantern' slides, whilst its last meeting before the move to St Bride's involved a steamer trip in June 1902 to the Holy Loch for a picnic. Some ladies had taken their bicycles with them on the boat, and went for a cycle, whilst others played a game of rounders with an orange! The party had to run, (which was regarded as being very undignified), to catch the boat back. The first Guild meeting in St Bride's was held on 29 November 1902, and in March 1903, 'Old Girls' presented a short operetta entitled *The Japanese Girls* to an audience that included members of The Park School Science Association. June 1903 saw another picnic outing, this time to Loch Dochart near Crianlarich, whilst in December 1903 a dance was held in the new St Bride's Hall, which was decorated with palms and other plants. Over 100 members and guests attended.

Whilst the Guild was rapidly becoming an important part of the School, with its growing number of former pupils, St Bride's itself also had an expanding roll. At the Prize-Giving held in the Hall in the summer of 1904, however, Miss Renton remarked that whilst the work of the School had reached a high standard, '. . . it had not yet reached the standard that was aimed at.' Thus she revealed one of her dominant characteristics: never to accept anything less than the very best. The School had engaged its first teacher of PE for the following session, and meanwhile the girls gave the 'fashionable gathering' assembled in the Hall an '. . . excellent exhibition of Swedish drill, performed . . . with much grace and skill'. ('Swedish drill' involved marching, stretching and bending to music.)

Guild Meetings continued, with readings from Browning, Dickens, Stevenson and Mrs

Gaskell, and a debate on the subject 'Is Athleticism Carried to Excess?', whilst the Prize-Giving of 1905 was held 'under the trees on the west lawn', when the girls '. . . marched out and took their places on the benches'. Miss Renton was again able to report an increased roll, and stressed that whilst the Scottish Education Department Leaving Certificate had been taken in English, French and Maths the previous year, '. . . lessons after all come second; . . . truthfulness, obedience, service, courtesy in . . . daily life come first.' The Headmistress also mentioned that a 'prominent place' had been given during that session to sewing, which was '. . . so essentially a woman's subject' that she was 'determined to

The end of the first session in St Bride's, 1903.
The entire school outside the front door; Miss Renton is on the extreme right, fifth row back.

have it raised to a higher standard'. Additionally, 'physical drill had received special attention . . .', whilst 'the proportion of music prizes was distinctly large . . .'. Medals were presented by Miss Cramb, of Hermitage House, and Mr Moir, representing the Girls' School Company, commented on St Brides' good fortune in possessing such 'beautiful grounds' and a fine Hall, which the other two schools belonging to the Company could only envy. In some respects, St Bride's was 'taking the lead'. The day concluded with tea being taken in the grounds, whilst there was also an exhibition of pupils' drawings, sewing, science diagrams and kindergarten handwork in the School.

In 1906 the Guild hosted a Shakespearean Recital, given by Graham Price of the Athenaeum, and a dramatic and social evening, during which *Pride and Prejudice* was acted by pupils and staff. Representatives of both The Park and St Columba's attended the evening, which concluded with a dance and the singing of the National Anthem. The summer also saw a picnic outing to Rowardennan, when some of the party climbed Ben Lomond, no easy feat in the long skirts of the time. At the Prize-Giving, according to *The*

An early 1900s St Bride's primary class.
This was Mr Taylor's Geography Room on the ground floor, with the display cabinet at the far end of the room still in place, at the time of the 1997 fire. In keeping with Miss Renton's aims, needlework is in progress.

26

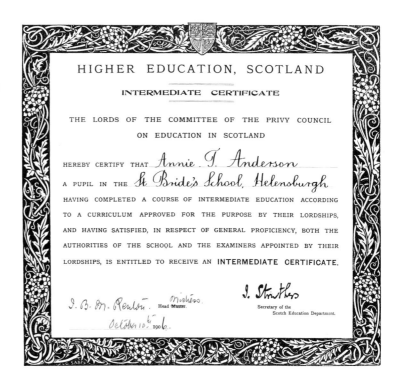

The Intermediate Certificate presented to Annie (Nance) Anderson in 1906. The following year she achieved her Leaving Certificate in French and English. Miss Anderson later returned to teach at St Bride's.
(See photo p. 46.)

Helensburgh and Gareloch Times, '. . . a large and fashionable company assembled in the Hall'. Miss Renton was able to report that there were now 120 pupils on the roll, including 18 boarders and twenty from outside Helensburgh who travelled by boat or train. Additional Maths and Science staff had been appointed to cope with the increasing roll. The Headmistress emphasised, as Mr A. Lindsay of the Girls' School Company had also done at Prize-Giving two years previously, that the School did not favour 'cramming of any kind'. Whilst the Leaving Certificate had led to a 'higher standard of general cultivation', the development of character was still paramount. Regrettably, according to Miss Renton:

> . . . the home preparation of the Middle School has distinctly suffered from the restless excitement which is the spirit of the age . . . happiness is rapidly becoming synonymous with excitement . . . amusements are pleasures only when there is a strong element of excitement in them (which) must in the course of time affect . . . home life.

Whilst making clear her priorities, Miss Renton was also able to report on the fact that former pupil Joan Hughes had graduated in English from the University of Glasgow, whilst the previous session's Head Girl, Isabel Inglis, was studying medicine there. Another former pupil, Moira McPhee, was at Oxford.

In 1907, the Guild held a 'Schumann Evening', which was attended by over 170 people, whilst in the summer, the last few of the original girls who had entered Helensburgh High School in 1895 left St Bride's, having, as Miss Renton said at Prize-Giving, 'grown up amongst us'. These girls were, she said:

27

St Bride's Sixth Form, 1907.

'Corbietree' in 2000. (Photo: Mrs E. Maclean.)

The Hockey Team, 1907, on the steps of St Bride's.

. . . dependable, loyal and warm-hearted . . . we are feeling sad. I thank the parents
of these girls for leaving their daughters with us throughout their whole school
career.

The girls had strengthened the School's traditions of 'honour, courtesy and loyalty.'

Miss Renton went on to announce the opening of a junior boarding-house, (almost
certainly Corbietree at 5 Upper Sutherland Crescent), and also commented on the fact
that the Scottish Education Department was '. . . pressing the claims of Science to . . . an
undue extent', stating that she had sent a letter of 'courteous protest', pointing out that
such emphasis affected the teaching of a second language (Latin or German in addition to
French). The Headmistress stated, however, that she was prepared to:

. . . devote a little more time to Science, (whilst) omitting it from the homework
timetable, to fit up a science room and to offer an interesting syllabus of observational
science (nature work and botany) in the lower forms, and . . . experimental science
in the middle forms.

Miss Renton also remarked on the newly-appointed Physical Education teacher, Miss
Douglas, who was:

... thoroughly competent to undertake special medical gymnastics ... There are girls who from time to time, owing to rapid growth, benefit greatly from two or three courses of special treatment.

There would also be 'optional drill' on Saturday mornings.

Miss Renton concluded by complimenting her staff, who had 'supported (her) organisation with unsparing zeal'.

The theme of the 'immense impetus' being given by the School to Physical Education was continued in the Headmistress's Report at Prize-Giving in 1908, when she thanked the 'medical men' for their support of physical training. 'Courses of special treatment' had been carried out 'under the direction of ... the doctors of the town (who) had co-operated most helpfully'. Miss Renton went on to warn parents that:

... School training should be supplemented by watchfulness at home in habits of sitting and walking, in the attendance at prep., music practice, etc. We want the girls to hold themselves well and to walk well.

There were apparently still a few parents who were against games for girls, but Miss Renton felt that:

The old gymnasium which today is the Music Studio.
This building was the coach-house and stables of Ardenlee when it was built in 1859.

. . . where the spirit of the School is against roughness and slangy talk there is nothing better than organised games for developing in girls unselfishness, self-control, obedience, thoughtfulness and good manners generally.

In support of this view, the Headmistress complimented the 'capital spirit' of the girls who came by train to attend Saturday morning games' practices. Meanwhile, plans had been drawn up to link the old coach-house, (the gymnasium, now the Music Studio, to the main building, as previously described. Paterson's plans were displayed in the entrance hall, and the Girls' School Company appealed for loans (at 3 per cent interest) to meet the estimated cost of £1,500–£2,000, which would provide a science laboratory and music rooms within the link.

Miss Renton was also able to report that ten girls had again passed the Intermediate Leaving Certificate of the Scottish Education Department. However, she had another warning for pupils and parents:

The English Department encourages good reading and the cultivation of taste . . . if a girl in her leisure-hour reading devotes herself to trashy stories . . . she need not think of this certificate.

Two hours a week were now being devoted to Science (instead of the three hours recommended by the S.E.D.) to allow girls to take two languages, which the Headmistress obviously regarded as being more important; three girls were now taking Greek. Meanwhile, teachers' salaries were £120 per annum.

1909 saw Guild members perform a *Rip Van Winkle* operetta, and they also gave a play-reading which was attended by more than 100 people. In December the Guild held their second reunion, at which S.6 girls performed the final scene from *The Merchant of Venice* and Guild members acted some scenes from *Nicholas Nickleby*. Supper in the gymnasium was followed by dancing. Guests were able to view the new corridors, cloakrooms and classrooms that had been constructed that year, making St Bride's, so Miss Renton claimed, 'second to none in equipment and accommodation'. One late afternoon per week was being given over to Science work in the new laboratory in the case of Middle and Upper School girls, whilst school now began ten minutes later in the mornings to allow girls to arrive on time by train. Reports were issued every term, and Assemblies were held every Monday morning, as they are in 2003. Miss Renton regretted the small size of the preparatory department, which, despite the move to St Bride's, she still felt was due to the distance which very young children would have had to walk to School.

In 1910 the Guild published their third *Annual Report* of their activities, and a pupil, Dorothy McGossan, produced and circulated a manuscript recording the School's activities. This has unfortunately not survived, but it was the forerunner of the *Guild Magazine* that would be published for the first time the following year, and which would run without a break until 1969. It is from these magazines, and subsequent *Lomond Annals*, in addition to the *Lomond Association Newspaper*s of 1979–1998, that material for this book is largely drawn.

The old Science laboratory which became the new Music room.
It was a Geography room before the 1997 fire.

St Bride's without its balcony, between 1902 and 1912.

The Prize-Giving of 1910 was again held in the School grounds, tea being taken on the lawn. Miss Renton referred to the steady growth of the School, but pointed out that the available pupil resources in Helensburgh had probably already been tapped; therefore any further increase in the roll would have to come from boarders. (Unfortunately it would be the First World War that would provide the upsurge in boarding numbers that the Headmistress wanted.) She appealed to those present to make the School known to a wider circle.

Whilst Miss Renton was able to report that another girl had gained entry to Oxford, she also gave news of a major development in the curriculum of the School for less-academic girls. A 'Domestic Science and Housewifery Department' had opened in September for girls over 17 who were not preparing for University. The Department would provide tuition in '. . . what pertains to the right ordering of a home', enabling the girls to 'take up such duties in a competent and earnest manner'. A 'fully-trained and experienced residential mistress' had been appointed, and she would give demonstration and practical lessons each week in 'plain cookery, advanced needlework, simple blouse and skirt-making, home nursing and first-aid, laundry-work, housewifery and home management'. Interestingly, however, Miss Melville, Mistress of Queen Margaret College in Glasgow, who was presenting the prizes, also stressed the need for women to strike out into fresh fields of activity and to show enterprise.

Also in 1910, the Guild gave a concert in aid of the Victoria Infirmary and the Aberfoyle Cot; charity-work was important to the School and would remain so throughout its history. Meanwhile, Mlle Humbert, who had been at the School since it opened, returned to Switzerland. She was presented with a purse of 15 sovereigns (a coin worth £1) and an inscribed gold watch. On the games' field, the St Bride's girls held their first recorded cricket match against the boys of Larchfield. After Larchfield had made 77 runs, St Bride's were dismissed for 12, 'due to the overhand (overarm) bowling, to which the girls were quite unaccustomed'.

By 1911, St Bride's had a staff of 16, all female and all unmarried, as women had to resign their posts upon marriage. There were six pupils in S.6. Plans were afoot to rebuild the balcony over the front door, which had been removed when A. N. Paterson's alterations were made a few years previously. It was estimated that this project would cost around £40, and an Appeal was launched with subscriptions of between 2/6d (12.5p) and a guinea (£1.05p) invited. It was felt that the restoration of the balcony would be a suitable way to mark the Coronation of King George V, but in addition a flag-pole was erected near to the front door, and a Union Jack, presented by a parent, Mr Lewis, was flown for the first time on Coronation Day itself, (22 June). The unfurling ceremony was performed by Dr Sewell, one of the Directors. The *Guild Magazine* reported that:

> In spite of the heavy rain, the whole School stood in file facing the new flag-staff at the salute, and sang the National Anthem. Afterwards they marched indoors, where the presentation of Coronation Medals took place.

These years leading up to World War One seemed notable for a spirit of British patriotism that is perhaps no longer in evidence; Trafalgar Day (21 October) was celebrated in a 'spirit of gratitude and patriotism', as was Empire Day on 24 May.

Prize -Giving was held in the Hall on 23 June. All the form-rooms were decorated for the occasion, and the School Hymn, Rinkart's 'Now Thank We All Our God' was sung. This hymn was apparently very dear to Miss Renton's heart, and it was still sung at Lomond's end-of-term assemblies until hymn-singing ceased in 2002.

1911 was also a notable year due to the bequest of Miss Cramb, who lived at Hermitage House where Hermitage Park is today. She left the then huge sum of £500 to provide bursaries to the School, together with a Dux Medal and annual prizes for Music and Art. Today, Lomond's S.5 subject prizes are still known as 'Cramb Awards', as are the School's Service Prizes for P.E. and the School Captain. On Miss Cramb's death in 1911, Hermitage House and grounds were purchased by the Town Council for £3,750. During World War One, the house was used as an auxiliary hospital; it then became an annexe for the primary department of Hermitage School (which had itself been built on land gifted to the town by Miss Cramb), until the opening of the new school in 1926. Subsequently, plans were made to turn the house into a library or museum, but, unfortunately, these were never realised, and after lying empty for a number of years, the house was demolished in 1963. Miss Cramb's walled garden stood on the site of the present War Memorial, and there was a mill-pond where the tennis-courts now are. She owned all the land that stretched from Victoria Road to Argyll Street.

At Prize-Giving, Miss Renton spoke of her greater confidence in 'the development of the important boarding element in the School', but also emphasised her desire that the girls should show 'a much stronger sense of duty and respectability' in their work, showing always 'thoroughness in little things'.

St Bride's with the newly-erected balcony over the front doors, post 1912, and pre-1923, as the new wing had not yet been built.
(Note the growth of the ivy since the picture on p32 was taken.)

In the new Domestic Science Department, 'cookery took the form of dinners', and included roasting, boiling, baking and frying. In keeping with the aims of the new Department, the Rev. Munro, who presented the prizes, urged the girls to put duty before pleasure, and to make the home 'the centre of unselfish service'. Perhaps paradoxically, however, St Bride's was already preparing its girls for University and for careers of their own.

By 1912, the Balcony Fund had still not reached halfway to its target, the total collected being £17 4/- (£17.20p.), whilst it had been decided to use part of the Cramb bequest to fund the university fees of a day pupil for two or three years with a bursary of £15 per annum. The first recipient was May Cunliffe, who had taken the Leaving Certificate in five subjects. Dux medals would also be provided from the fund. The Prize-Giving, on 19 June, was notable for being the wettest since the School was formed in 1895, and this weather was continued into the monsoon winter of 1913, which saw the Dumbarton–Helensburgh railway line washed away. The girls dressed sensibly in 'oilskins and sou'westers' (which today's fashion-conscious children might more readily associate with the deck of a trawler!). The awful winter made the balcony even more of a necessity if callers at the front door were to avoid a soaking, and with the help of a £6.00 donation from Guild members, and £10.00 from the Directors, the fund reached the total of £48 10/- (£48.50p) and the balcony was erected.

Also in 1913, flowering trees, now a Helensburgh trademark, were planted along the streets surrounding the School on the instigation of Dr E. Hunter, a town councillor: white lilacs in Millig Street, laburnums in Sinclair Street (these had to be removed after a child ate some seeds and became seriously ill), and flowering cherries in Colquhoun Street. Meanwhile, Guild members voted to fund a cot at Strathblane Children's Home, a

Strathblane Children's Home in 1925.
A cot was funded by St Bride's from 1913–1948.

St Bride's in 1913.
Photographed from the west corner of the front lawn, (now the car park). The only surviving part of the building is on the extreme left—the 2003 Music Studio, the former coach-house of Ardenlee.

The Dining Hall at St Bride's in 1913.
At the time of the 1997 fire, this room was occupied by the Bursar's offices.

charitable cause that the School was to support for 35 years at Strathblane, and for a further 20 years at Maryhill. The School roll reached 150, and a new junior boarding-house, Birdston, in West Clyde Street on the site of the present Commodore Hotel, was opened to replace Corbietree in Upper Sutherland Crescent. It was used by the school until 1916. At this time, fees were £15.00 per annum for day pupils, and for boarders between 70 and 85 guineas (£73.50p and £89.25p). An additional guinea (£1.05p) was charged annually for books, stationery and drawing materials. There were also extra charges of between one and three guineas a term for individual tuition in piano, violin, singing, elocution, dancing, needlework, swimming, riding and 'mechancial gymnastics', plus a further charge of a guinea a week in the event of 'infectious illness', to include 'special nursing'.

During the year, Miss Renton appeared as both Prospero and Cardinal Wolsey at Guild play-readings, whilst at Prize-Giving, nearly everyone wore a wild rose to celebrate Alexandra Day (26 June).

World War One

1914 was marked by the death of Miss G Kinnear, first Headmistress of The Park School, who had been born in 1828, and who had not retired until she was 72, in 1900. Meanwhile at Prize-Giving, Miss Renton reported on the School's 'excellent enrolments', which could not be further increased until the boarding-house question was solved: 'Upon the solution of this problem depended the permanent success of the School.' (Corbietree and Birdston had almost certainly been rented.)

Shandon Hydro.

Boarders' tennis on the lawn at High Mayfield.

Mayfield in 2000. (Photo: Mrs E. Maclean.)

Also in 1914, the School's use of Shandon Hydro swimming-pool began, whilst sports were also held at St Bride's for the first time. (Old Girls both organised the event and participated, whilst Miss Renton presented cups and other prizes in the Hall), and there were plans for a School Museum; items received included a snake-skin and a 'classified collection of eggs'. Term Two saw an 'amount of epidemic illness unheard of in the history of the School'. Those affected by the unspecified illness included the Headmistress, but by Prize-Giving Day in June she had recovered sufficiently to reiterate strongly that, in her view, the girls did not show:

> . . . anything like sufficient individual responsibility. (It is) far too hard a struggle to obtain . . . thorough work. (They are) content with far too low a standard of accuracy. The supreme importance of accuracy is what (I) wish to emphasise. (It will) . . . develop character and prepare the girls to meet the difficulties of life.

In 1915, High Mayfield in Havelock Street, round the corner from Kinnear House, was rented and became the third boarding-house and also the home of Domestic Science, as families dislocated by the First World War sought stability for their children in a relatively safe area. St Bride's participated vigorously in the war-effort, holding a sale of work for hospitals, which raised over £100, and collecting sphagnum moss in Glen Fruin for use as absorbent dressings: 'First of all the twigs and grass were carefully picked out of it.' A 'Patriotic Club' was also flourishing in School, furthering the study of patriotic verse and the growth of the Empire. Miss Renton was proud that her girls were being trained in the '. . . highest ideals of patriotism and citizenship'.

The year was also notable for the death of the Chairman of the Board of Directors of the Girls' School Company, The Rev. Principal Lindsay. He had held this position almost since the Company's inception, and was succeeded by Mr J.A. Spens. Meanwhile, fifteen boys were in the Preparatory Department, along with an equal number of girls; most of the boys would proceed to Larchfield when they were old enough. 'Water Sports' were held for the first time at Shandon Hydro, and the girls of St Bride's played a cricket match against those of St George's School in Edinburgh. (Needless to say, it rained!) There were three cricket teams in St Bride's at the time, known as 'The Roaring Forties', 'The Boisterous Bow-Wows' and 'The Hopeful Leather-Hunters'.

Miss Renton was keen to establish a new senior boarding-house that would cater specifically for the girls who were following the Domestic Science course, but any construction-work was out of the question during the War. The course was proving very popular, since, according to the Headmistress, parents were keen for their daughters to 'train for something'. Eight girls obtained the Intermediate Leaving Certificate, and one the Full Certificate, although Miss Renton again emphasised that '. . . the School does not by any means concentrate on preparing for examinations'. In fact, some girls 'for reasons of health' attended School for only half a day or perhaps had no homework.

The School reached its Twenty-First birthday in the middle of the 'War to End All Wars'. (Ironically, it would reach its Golden Jubilee at the end of World War Two.) Miss Renton considered it inappropriate to hold any kind of celebration in 1916, although a

1916: *Under the Quicken Tree*—Pageant of St Bride, written by Miss E. Beale.

pageant based on the life of St Bride, written by a 'friend of the School', Miss Evelyn Beale, was performed by the girls. (As has already been mentioned, Miss Beale was later to design the plaque depicting St Bride that is still to be seen in the Bridesian Library. Instead, a number of fund-raising events were held to help the War effort, including the Scottish Women's Hospital in Serbia. The 'Patriotic Club' sent over 50 parcels of clothing, tobacco, books and magazines to soldiers in the Persian Gulf and the Dardanelles, and to friends or relations of pupils and staff in France, whilst each class 'adopted' a Prisoner of War in Germany, sending him fortnightly parcels. In addition, £37 was paid to insure the School against 'aircraft damage'. Meanwhile, at Prize-Giving in June, Miss Renton referred to a number of St Bride's 'Old Boys' from the Preparatory Department who had 'made the supreme sacrifice'.

The First World War was proving, however, that women were capable of assuming roles that had previously been the preserve of males. In a letter to Guild members in May, the Headmistress referred to the fact that St Bride's girls now had 'opportunities and interests . . . not in the option of our "originals" of 1895'. She felt that:

> . . . girls of today have to be trained to realise that women must be ready to meet any emergency in the years to come . . . . Women's work at the present time is of extraordinary interest to me.

The Headmistress stressed, however, that the early days of the School had 'shaped traditions . . . binding us together by common principles of reverence, courtesy and loyalty'. At Prize-Giving, Miss Renton again commented on two factors which she felt would always affect the School's potential for growth. One was the '. . . limitations of possible enrolments due to the geographical position and size of the town . . .', whilst the other was '. . . the exceptional number of short enrolments due to families coming to the town for brief periods'. It could be argued that both of these factors still affect Lomond over 86 years later. However, the roll was holding steady at 150, with 40 boarders enrolled for the following session, despite the 10 per cent salary increase awarded to the Company's teachers, which led to a fee-increase. In fact, the rapid increase in demand for boarding places that had been fuelled by the War led to a long lease being taken out by the Company on Ashmount in Millig Street, (now the home of Lomond's Headmaster, Mr Angus Macdonald) to house junior boarders and to replace Birdston. Ashmount had been built in 1865, and in 1869 was owned by Mr T. Gallie, but by 1875 it had become a school run by the Misses Mary and Margaret Murdoch, which continued to operate until c.1903. In addition, Birkhall in Havelock Street was purchased for use as a sanatorium and an 'overflow' boarding-house, whilst the Domestic Science Department was also relocated here. In her book *From the Alleghenies to the Hebrides* Margaret Fay Shaw recalls the dreadful chilblains that the girls suffered at Birkhall, both on their hands and feet, and the agony of trying to squeeze their feet into their heavy brogue shoes. She also mentions the 'crocodile', (two by two), walks up the Old Luss Road to see Loch Lomond, the Crianlarich hills, and highland cows in the fields.

The year was also notable for the death of the School cat, Ginger, who was an unofficial mascot. Ginger had unfortunately succumbed to poisoning, but his position was quickly filled by 'Ginger Junior'.

1917 saw a rapid increase in the School roll as the War continued, despite further salary and fee increases, which were to be repeated in 1919, 1920 and 1921. St Bride's now had 180 pupils, including over 60 boarders, who were living in Kinnear House, Ashmount, High Mayfield and Birkhall (both in Havelock Street). There were five classes in the Lower School, and the Preparatory Department was the largest ever. A measles epidemic swept the School, and Chapelfield at 33 East Argyle Street with its four-poster beds was enlisted as an emergency sanatorium.

Miss Renton referred at Prize-Giving to education as 'war-work of a great kind', and stated that the School's aim was '. . . first and foremost to educate girls so that they might become capable women with high ideals of life . . .', whilst Lord Strathclyde, presenting the prize-certificates, (all prize-money had been donated to charity), suggested that in teachers' hands 'lay the destiny of the country'. He urged the girls to do, in the holidays, '. . . something for their native land in its hour of need . . . to take their share in bearing the heat and burden of the day'. Meanwhile, Prof. G Gibson succeeded Mr Spens as Chairman of the Girls' School Company.

In 1918, Burnbrae, which had been built, like Ardenlee, in 1859, was purchased from Mr Peter Miller as another senior boarding-house for 30 girls, as the roll had now increased to 190. Unfortunately, wartime conditions still made any building at St Bride's itself

Ashmount.

Birkhall in 2000. (Photo: Mrs E. Maclean.)

Burnbrae with its original roof.

impossible, and consequently two rooms at Burnbrae had to be used for the Preparatory Department. A 'flu epidemic closed the School for a time, with only 3 girls at Burnbrae escaping infection and almost the whole of Ashmount being confined to bed. (It may interest boarders in 2003 to know that in 1918, Ashmount girls were allowed into town once every three weeks to spend their pocket money of 4d. [less than 2p.] per week.) The long-awaited Armistice was celebrated by the singing of The National Anthem and The Marseilles on the front lawn, and a 'Kipling Night' was held. Over £250, raised by collections, concerts, plays and lectures, as well as prize-money from Prize-Giving, was donated to various charities. Meanwhile, the Education (Scotland) Act standardised teachers' salary-scales.

Miss Renton's Last Decade at St Bride's

By 1919, the roll had grown further to 200, including 80 boarders, which was considered by Miss Renton to be the optimum size, allowing for a good spread of subjects to be taught. Birkfell in Charlotte Street was being used as an additional boarding-house, and boarding places were full a year ahead. Forty pupils were on the Preparatory roll, whilst another flu epidemic saw the School closed for 7 working days. Interestingly, at this time the Girls' School Company had produced a booklet, to be sent out to parents, entitled *Regulations For The Prevention of the Spread of Infectious Diseases*. It stipulated that certificates, signed by parents or guardians, had to be shown to the Headmistress at the start of term, stating that to the best of parents' knowledge, the girl had not 'FOR AT LEAST THREE WEEKS been exposed to any infectious disease, nor entered any house where such disease existed'. Any pupils who had been exposed to infectious illness could not return to School

The staff outside Burnbrae, 1919.
Miss Renton is centre of back row.

St Bride's School staff, 1919.
Misses—*standing:* Wellwood, Hamilton, Edwards, Lornie, Cartmel, Anderson, Grace.
Seated: Maxwell, Still, White, Jack, Renton, Harrison, Preston, Snell.

without a medical certificate showing that they had complied with the conditions in the booklet.

Infectious Diseases were divided into Three classes:

Class One: Diphtheria, Scarlet Fever, Smallpox and Typhoid Fever.

Class Two: Measles, German Measles, Chicken Pox, Whooping-Cough, Mumps.

Class Three: Ringworm.

The Headmistress had the power to suspend classes, or the attendance of particular pupils, if she considered that an epidemic could be thus prevented. In the case of Typhoid and Scarlet Fever, girls who had been infected could not return to School for at least six weeks, provided, in the case of the latter disease, that there were no 'suppurating glands'; in the case of Smallpox that 'the skin lesions have all healed', and in the case of Diphtheria that there was 'no longer any . . . abnormal discharge from the throat, nose, ears or eyes'.

The booklet also listed quarantine periods, which were over three weeks long in some cases. No clothing, hair-brushes etc. used by girls with a Class One disease could be brought to School, whilst no books used by girls with any of the listed diseases could be used in School, and had to be destroyed. All clothes and other personal articles had to be disinfected in the case of a Class Two or Three disease.

Meanwhile, at Prize-Giving, Miss Renton reminded the girls that they had 'a heritage from those who had died for their country', and stated that they must be 'trained worthily, with a high sense of duty, and with . . . an ideal of social service.'

The Dux pupils of both 1919 and 1920, (Rhona Adam and Elspeth Ure), gained places at Cambridge, and in the enlightened fashion that seems to have been typical of Miss Renton, German, which was compulsory at Cambridge, was also strongly emphasised at St Bride's. Miss Renton commented that, '. . . for many reasons we ought to make it our business to encourage our young people to study the language of our late enemies'. The Headmistress also stressed the importance of the School's Domestic Science Department, stating that every girl who left the sixth-form should '. . . be able to do anything whatsoever in a house and at the same time . . . be an interesting woman'. Domestic skills were linked to patriotic duty too, Miss Renton commenting that the more girls could be trained in '. . . the practical politics of home life in these difficult days, the more work we are doing for our country'.

The end of The Great War and a continuing influx of new pupils as families attempted to get back to normal after the Armistice, led to the announcement of plans for new classrooms and an Art Studio. These were to be built 'as expeditiously as possible'. Two thousand pounds of debentures were sold within a few days. Meanwhile, despite the cramped conditions in St Bride's itself, the good relationship between staff and pupils which still characterizes Lomond today was commented upon by a Scandinavian pupil, Hanne Halliesen:

I have never seen or heard about teachers being so kind in explaining things as the teachers do here . . . teachers (are) much liked because of the interest they show in the children. How can a girl dislike a person who always smiles and who is always ready to help and make the children happy?

Burnbrae girls on their annual picnic, 1920.

1st St Bride's Girl Guides' Company, 1921.
Miss Nance Anderson, centre.

At this burgeoning point in the School's development, facilities for games were obviously at a premium. As they had been in 1895, games were still played on the lawn at the front of Kinnear House; on the field at the back of St Bride's where the gymnasium and the science-block now stand, from 1917 on the Larchfield School playing-fields, (Lomond's present rugby pitches), and also on the ground by the former curling-pond at the east end of Havelock Street. In 1921, a new pavilion was erected by St Bride's on the Larchfield playing-fields at a cost of £621 to mark the School's 25th Anniversary. The pavilion, which was green with a black roof, and possessed a 'most superior veranda', was a reconstructed army hut. A Christmas Fair raised almost half the cost, and an oak table for the pavilion was presented by the Guild. Additionally, a 40-feet flag-pole together with a flag depicting St Bride was presented by Mr and Mrs Carstairs of Karachi, who had a daughter at the School.

In 1921, Kildare Lodge, (formerly called Ellangowan, opposite Larchfield), in Colquhoun Street, with its 'lovely garden and glorious views' had been purchased to act as the sanatorium, whilst Birkhall had become a fully-fledged boarding-house. High Mayfield had also been purchased outright, as boarding numbers had increased to 90. However, the planned extension to St Bride's had been temporarily shelved as being too costly, perhaps because of the expenditure on boarding-houses. Links with the present include the shorter afternoon hours which were introduced to allow more light for organised games after school, and the fact that a number of girls remained at St Bride's from the age of 5 until they left at 17. Burnbrae's 15 hens laid 700 eggs during the year; the School Orchestra was founded, whilst Teachers' salaries were £230 per annum, and were paid termly, rather than monthly.

Kildare Lodge in 2000. (Photo: Mrs E. Maclean.)

The Sixth Form in 1922.
Back row: M. Reid, D. Roberts, M. Dron, J. Holmes. *Middle row:* C. Cairns, M. Hearn,
J. Dick-Cleland, J. Brown, J. Stockdale. *Front row:* E. Milne, I. McMorran.

The site to the rear of the new (1923) East Wing, before building work commenced.
Today, the Biology laboratories occupy this position.

1922 saw a day's holiday for Princess Mary's wedding day, and also the foundation of an S.6 Literary and Debating Society. Motions included: 'A Poet is of More Use Than A Plumber'; 'The Age at Which Women Obtain the Suffrage Should be Lowered'; 'Games Should Not be Played on a Sunday', and 'In Norse Mythology There is a Greater Element of the Divine Than in the Greek'. (This might be a very short debate in 2003!)

Amongst the hens at Burnbrae the girls managed to play tennis, croquet and clock-golf, whilst at Birkhall the Domestic Science pupils made 'test dinners' and entertained the Headmistress and the Directors to a seven-course meal. In her speech at Prize-Giving, Miss Renton reiterated that whilst many leavers obtained places at university, most 'passed into home life'. Therefore the School had:

> . . . the definite aim of training . . . girls to be high-minded, unselfish women, . . . showing in their own homes that they can radiate happiness . . . eager to give their talents and time to social service.

By June 1923, funds had finally been found to commence work on the new wing, which today houses Lomond's English Department, the Library, and Mrs Brown's Transitus room, having survived the 1997 fire. The wing bears the date 1923, although it was not in fact opened until the following year. In words that could have been written in 1998, Miss King, Head of English and Editor of *The Bridesian*, remarked that:

> Ours is the privilege of watching the visionary hopes . . . materialise . . . There is something extraordinarily fascinating about a new building; it embodies so much, since so often it is the concrete expression of the ideal . . . evolved from energy which is extremely practical but at the same time intensely spiritual.

It was estimated that the new wing (designed once again by Alexander Paterson) would cost £6,000. Originally there were plans for one storey only, but Miss Renton, always a visionary, dreamed of a second storey to provide a library and reading-room which would become a 'temple of quiet and study'. There were also to be some alterations to the main building, including the enlargement of the dining-room, (the room which before the 1997 fire was occupied by the Bursar's offices). Donations flowed in from parents (one donating the then huge sum of £250); Sir William Raeburn (£50), and individual officers of The Guild. Another £50 came from Guild funds. Miss Renton expressed the hope that the new facilities would encourage girls to stay on into S.6, as, in another echo of the more recent past, she lamented the 'fashion' for St Bride's girls to be sent away elsewhere to board in the sixth form. In another effort to recruit pupils, fees were reduced in the Preparatory School to encourage parents to send their children to the School at a younger age. Meanwhile, the School acquired its first gramophone, and the bus-rides to Shandon Hydro's swimming-baths were described as being 'always in the nature of an adventure', perhaps due to the unreliability of the buses. Fees for day-pupils had risen to 15 guineas (£15.75) per annum for the kindergarten and 39 guineas (£40.95) for S.6.

It is true to say that 1924 was almost as momentous a year in the life of St Bride's as 1998 was for Lomond. Firstly, Lansdowne Park built in 1857, (first occupied by Patrick Stead, brewer), and its beautiful grounds was purchased from the Aitken family (although it was not in fact occupied by boarders until January 1925). Lansdowne became the senior girls' boarding-house, and Miss Renton became its first House Mistress; this acquisition reflected the continuing growth in demand for boarding places; numbers had topped 100 in the boarding-houses, whilst the total roll was 230. The Domestic Science Department was also relocated to Lansdowne, where the grounds also provided the girls with opportunities for botany and rock-gardening. The latter pursuit became quite a craze for a few years, with departing girls gifting rock-plants, instead of books, for the Lansdowne library.

Although there were many delays in the completion of the new wing, one of which was caused by Miss Renton's insistence, when the building was apparently finished, that a window be inserted in the east wall of what is now Dr Everett's English classroom, as the room was too dark, with only one window at the far end. This alteration was to be made regardless of cost, and the window, which today looks out on the landscaped garden area to the east of the school, became known as 'The £200 Window'! The building was open for inspection on Prize-Giving Day in June 1924, when 'the spacious (Art) studio' (Mrs Brown's Transitus room in 2003) and the large, airy classrooms, (today the English Department) excited the admiration of all.' The new library (in 2003 the Bridesian Library) was also to be the headquarters of the Old Girls' Guild, serving as a club-room and meeting-place.

Beginnings of the new wing—Autumn 1923.
(Sketch: J.L. Anderson, S.6., 1923.)

50

The grounds of Lansdowne Park in 1925.

Lansdowne Park, 1925.

Lansdowne Park, south view, 1925.

TELEPHONE Nº 956 DOUGLAS.

A. N. PATERSON & STODDART,

ARCHITECTS.

LATE CAMPBELL DOUGLAS & PATERSON.

ALEXANDER N. PATERSON, M.A, A.R.S.A.,
F.R.I.B.A.
D. McKAY STODDART,
LICENTIATE R.I.B.A.

266 St VINCENT STREET,

GLASGOW,

10th November 1924.

My dear Miss Swinburne,

In view of your sudden and overwhelming sorrow in the death of your dear mother you will not, I hope, think it unfeeling that I should write to you about business.

But, if, as is likely, you are not to be present at the meeting to-day – if still to be held – it may save you trouble to learn that I was in touch with Miss Renton on Saturday and obtained her views as to the Writers whose busts should be selected, these being Shakespeare and Milton, Scott and Burns. That also would be my own selection. The decision on this point I can easily ascertain in Helensburgh, but should you still wish to see me on Friday aft. I shall be here about 2.30.

With this may I send you my very heart-felt sympathy and prayer for your support and consolation in your present trouble.

Yours faithfully,
Alexander N. Paterson

10 November 1924.

AN Paterson, architect of the 1923 East Wing, offers condolences to Mrs Swinburne for the death of her mother. He suggests that busts of Shakespeare, Milton, Scott and Burns be placed in the Bridesian Library upon its completion. Today, there are four plinths but only 2 busts. Were the four ever provided?

Opposite:
The Bridesian Library, 1924.
Still Lomond's Library nearly 80 years later.

The shelving and other panelling in this room cost around £600, a very large sum in 1924. The care which A. N. Paterson, despite illness which required a stay of 6 weeks in London for treatment, took with the design and decoration of the room is clear from 3 surviving letters, some several pages long, which he wrote to the Guild President, Miss E Swinburne, during the autumn and winter of 1923. In one of these letter, he remarked that:

> . . . the ceiling . . . the large and low-silled windows, the proportions of the room and its use . . . seem to call for a scheme having a certain element of dignity combined with comfort such as one gets in 18th Century interiors . . . .

The official opening of the new wing did not take place until 19 December 1924, and it was carried out by Mrs Isobel Gunn, (nee Ure) who had been the first pupil enrolled in the new Helensburgh High School back in Charlotte Street days. Mrs Gunn opened the Library door with a key tied in ribbons of the School colours, and Miss Beale's panel depicting St Bride was unveiled. A dance to celebrate the opening of the new wing was held in the Art Studio that evening. Miss Beale's *Pageant of St Bride*, was also performed, as it had been on the School's silver anniversary in 1916, St Bride herself being played by pupil Leslie Wareing, who went on to become a 1930s film-star. A huge number of Old Girls, from all over Britain and beyond, either attended the opening in person, or wrote to Miss Renton or Guild Officers enclosing donations to purchase books for the new Library. (It is also interesting to note that nearly 30 years into the School's life, there were already 46 former members of staff listed in *The Bridesian* magazine, living as far afield as Canada, South Africa and Australia.)

Miss Evelyn Beale's plaque of St Bride, unveiled in the Bridesian Library, 1924.

Burnbrae girls practise for the Ashmount croquet tournament, 1926.

By 1925, the new wing, including the Library, the Art Studio and three Music practice-rooms on the top floor, and classrooms and cloakrooms for the Preparatory Department downstairs, was fully operational. Outside, the tennis-court that disappeared under the new dining-hall in 1998 was laid out; it was played on for the last time in 1996, and so lasted almost exactly 70 years.

Elsewhere in the School, Ashmount was purchased outright, and extended; it also hosted a School croquet tournament, whilst the Burnbrae ducks and chickens produced over 900 eggs. Motions discussed by the Debating Society included: 'Scotland Should Have Home Rule'; 'School Uniform Should Be Worn On All Public Occasions', 'Children's Literature is Degenerating' and 'Science Dispels The Wonder and Magic of the World'. Pupils were praised (or humiliated) by having their marks publicly read out at Assembly at the end of every term, whilst also at Assembly, a 'new method of standing' was introduced, with juniors at the front and seniors at the rear. This 'new method' is still in use 75 years later, but one cannot help thinking that any other arrangement must have obscured the view of the youngest pupils! In June, the weather was kind for the annual Prize-Giving, which was held on the front lawn. Miss Renton commented on the importance of giving '. . . the non-academic girl the training and prestige that she is entitled to . . .', and also remarked on:

> . . . the restlessness of the age through the complete change in social habits since the War, (which is) strongly reflected in the child of today.

The Headmistress also paid tribute to the Housekeeper of St Bride's, Annie Downs, who had served at Kinnear House from its opening in 1895, and at St Bride's since 1902: 'Downs' (as she was known to distinguish her from another School servant, Annie McColl, who was always known as 'Annie', see photo p. 74) seems to have lived on site in the 'cottage' link constructed by Paterson to join Ardenlee to what is now the Music Studio. (This was demolished after the 1997 fire.) She was responsible for the production of School lunches every day.

1927 marked the 25th anniversary of the St Bride's site; to commemorate the event, Miss Renton presented the School with an engraved rose-bowl as a Form Conduct Trophy. It bore the text of her traditional end-of-term reading, which epitomises the ethos which she tried to instil into her girls:

> Whatsoever things are true, just, honourable, pure, lovely, of good report—think on these things.

Meanwhile an S.5 production of *As You Like It* raised funds both for new stage-curtains and for a donation to the newly-established Shakespeare Memorial Theatre at Stratford Upon Avon; the wet weather at the end of the summer term was blamed on an eclipse; the School badge was sewn onto the girls' Dexter hats to avoid confusion with the uniforms of other schools (apparently a perennial problem) and old St Bride's uniforms were sent to the Western Isles to help relieve poverty. The new wing was also opened at Ashmount, and an 18 hole putting-green was laid out at Lansdowne Park. Excursions included a visit

Miss Renton, centre, with the Preparatory School outside St Bride's, c.1927.
The new wing can be seen on the right, and the balcony is clearly visible in the centre.

to the Helensburgh Steam Laundry by the Domestic Science class, whilst in the Debating society, Jean Anderson argued that it was a '. . . Woman's Duty to Devote Her Entire Attention to Her Home, Because on Her Depended the Future of the Nation.' She was opposed by M. Cowie, who felt that girls were entitled to make careers for themselves. The year was also marked by the death of Dr Sewell, one of the original Directors of the School.

By 1928, Miss Renton was approaching retirement, and the School Captain, Edith Currie, launched an Appeal '. . . in acknowledgement of all that has been done for the School by Miss Renton and the staff . . .' and to reflect the pupils' gratitude to the Old Girls who had provided the Library. The idea of a personal gift from pupils had been rejected by Miss Renton for two years, presumably on the grounds of modesty, but on her eventual agreement in 1928, each girl donated 2/6d, (12½p.), in order, in the words of the Headmistress, '. . . that they themselves may have a share in giving something beautiful and lasting to the School'. The girls' legacy has been in St Bride's Hall for over 70 years, and fortunately survived the fire of 1997: a magnificent oak refectory table of Italianate design. The Directors presented an oak chair of similar design to accompany it, which also survived the fire. By this time in the School's evolution, the whole of the ground floor and the laboratory (a Geography room until Easter 1998 and now Mr I. Macdonald's Music room) had electric lighting, the installation of which had cost £149 10/6d (£149.52p). Gas-mantles were in use elsewhere in the School. The Hall stage had footlights, whilst the new

The playing-fields at the rear of St Bride's.
A girls' cricket match is in progress.
This site is now occupied by the Science Block, the Gymnasium and the playground.

Cricket Team, 1927–28.
Back row: Muriel Miller, Hazel McCrindle, Elizabeth MacLean, Kate Rickey.
Middle row: Berta Boag, Betty Beaumont, Jane Rickey (captain), Marjorie King, Peggy Hutton.
Front: Nancy McLeish, Alison Nicholson.

St Bride's Hall (c.1950), with the Italianate table and chair on the stage.

tennis courts at St Bride's and Lansdowne were formally opened by Miss Renton on 26 April; (a grass court already existed at Kinnear House). New 'sliding wall-bars' were also fitted to the gymnasium (the 2003 Music Studio). The Christmas Service, then as now attended by many former pupils, was held for the first time in the School Hall, and was described as '. . . one of the most impressive occasions that the Hall has ever witnessed'. Meanwhile, the Debating Society discussed the merits of introducing 'fagging', (i.e. junior pupils acting as servants for older ones).

In another link with the present, an Open Morning was held during the summer term, and must have paid dividends, since Miss Renton announced at Prize-Giving that the '. . . increased enrolments for the coming year would prove an embarrassing problem'. At Lansdowne, the girls leaving were asked to present books rather than rose-bushes, and the 'cobwebby and disused' rooms above the stables were converted to form a sitting-room for the House-staff and a study for sixth-form boarders. (In 2003 these rooms form part of the accommodation of Mrs Hassall, Lansdowne Housemistress, and her family.) At Burnbrae, 'hen monitors' had been appointed, and an 8 oz. trout was guddled from the burn in the grounds. The School roll had reached 220, and 120 boarders were shared between the five boarding-houses. Several former pupils were by this time on the staff, and Miss Renton, again ahead of her time, was expressing the wish that private sponsorship could provide scholarships, and that '. . . wealthy people interested in . . . education could be inspired to offer them'. (This wish found an echo in the 1990s when a number of overseas pupils were funded by the parents of existing Lomond pupils.) In 1928, only one competitive scholarship of £60.00 per year for a boarder was being offered, but in 1929 the number would be increased to three, and in 1930 to four. Miss Renton's appeal was supported by Mr Warr, who presented the prizes in 1928 and remarked that:

> The poor intelligentsia are the backbone of any nation, and they should be helped to educate their children in the best schools.

(Arguably, the Assisted Places scheme which ran throughout the 1990s, and which is currently being phased out, fulfilled the aims of Miss Renton and Mr Warr.) The latter also expressed the view that:

> Those who look on education merely as a means of wresting £ s d (money) from the world can only be stigmatized as intellectual barbarians.

In fact, the sum of £60 per year was quite a generous figure, since in 1928 the fees for Day Girls were six guineas (£6.30p.) per term for the Preparatory Department; 11 guineas, (£11.55p.) per term for the Lower School, and 13 guineas, (£13.65p.), for the Upper School. These rates had been unchanged since at least 1923. Boarding fees ranged from 120 guineas (£126) to 135 guineas (£141.75p.) per session, depending on the age of the child. There were, however, a number of 'extras' to be paid for, in particular a charge of 15/- (75p) per term for 'books, stationery and drawing materials' for Senior pupils; a similar amount for Laboratory fees to include use of science apparatus; a sum of between 2/6d (12 ½p.) and 5/- (25p.) for 'playground fees', plus, for boarders, 'personal laundry fees'. Additionally, all pupils were expected to provide a dictionary, a Bible, a hymn-book, atlas, paint-box, pastels and sewing materials. Individual lessons in Piano, Violin, Cello, Orchestra, Singing, Dancing, Elocution, Swimming, Riding, and 'Medical Gymnastics' cost between 7/6d (37½p.) and 5 guineas (£5 25p.) per term. Holidays, particularly the summer break of 10 weeks, were long, and were geared more to boarders than to day-pupils. Consequently, there were very few short breaks, like the present October-week holiday.

During 1928, St Bride's achieved something of a publicity coup when it was featured in *The Scottish Castle* magazine, which commented that the School:

> . . . charms even at first glance along the drive and across the lawn . . . it doesn't look like a school . . . it is infinitely more than a school . . .a spirit of service and of love.

Miss Renton was quoted in the article as saying that:

> . . . our training of the girls in character, our inspiring them with ideals of honour and unselfishness, our encouraging them to develop their leisure-time wisely, our interesting them in various activities, apart from actual lessons; our maintenance of the happy atmosphere that has always characterised St Bride's, depends upon the fact that I have behind me a loyal and devoted staff who do not spare themselves in the interests of the School.

Miss Renton's Retirement

1929 was a momentous year in the life of the School. The woman who had shaped it, guided it and devoted her life to it, retired. By this time 1500 girls had passed through the School, and, remarkably, every single one of Miss Renton's 34 years in charge had seen an increase in the roll; the Preparatory Department was the largest it had ever been, and entry to the School was possible only by selective test. Very few vacancies existed. Miss Renton had, as was stated in *The Helensburgh and Gareloch Times*, left 'a distinctive and indelible mark' on two generations. Tributes poured in from far and wide, and Old Bridesians from all over Britain assembled for Miss Renton's presentation ceremony in June. This was held in the School Hall, following the Prize-Giving, which was held for the first time in the Victoria Halls due to the number of Old Girls attending, forming the largest-ever audience in the Halls at that time. The balcony was reserved for Old Girls, but many had to stand in the aisles, wearing name-cards to show their maiden names and dates of attendance at St Bride's or at 'Helensburgh High School'. Among them were the School's first pupil, Isobel Gunn (Ure), and Miss Ethel Ross, then of Surrey, who had been the School's first boarding pupil in 1899. As the 'Old Girls' Guild' section of *The Bridesian* commented '. . . it was as a big family that we . . . met to honour Miss Renton'.

In her Prize-Giving speech, Miss Renton remarked that in many ways she was 'younger' in 1929 than she had been 34 years earlier, as where once she would have 'struck awe into the souls of the Junior school', she was now 'treated as a friend'. She went on to comment on the sense of 'social duty' revealed by the girls in their 'social and philanthropic work', which provided a 'religious education in the best sense of the word', cultivating in them a 'large-hearted generous attitude to life'.

Senior Burnbrae girls, 1929.

Turning to 'business' for the last time, Miss Renton commented on parental complaints about the frank nature of girls' reports:

> . . . it would be really quite easy for us to gloss over weaknesses and faults, but we just cannot do so, . . . and the consolation . . . is that a high standard in a School is a characteristic of which a parent ought to be proud.

In other speeches that day, Provost R. Herbertson agreed that 'public service seemed to be the tradition of the School . . . ', and that it was exemplified in Miss Renton herself, whilst 'An Appreciation' in the Guild section of *The Bridesian* commented that the Headmistress had been a 'pioneer' who had 'set out to give her girls as good an education as their brothers'. From the very first days at Helensburgh High School, Miss Renton had been determined that 'nothing should be done for show . . . (but) everything to make a good foundation'. She disliked academic specialisation, and had 'trained girls for living'. She had '. . . the secret of a youthful heart', and possessed a 'rare understanding', together with 'abounding vitality and ceaseless energy', putting 'principle before expediency', and inspiring in her pupils, 'first of all, respect'. She would always encourage them 'to do something, even though it were the most insignificant thing, rather than do nothing'. She shared this belief with the present Lomond Headmaster, Mr Angus Macdonald.

At St Bride's, after the Prize-Giving, Miss Renton was presented with a Georgian silver tea and coffee service by the staff, monogrammed with her initials, together with a mahogany tray and a crystal bowl. From pupils, past and present, she received a mahogany bookcase and five chairs, and a leather-bound signature-book that had been inscribed by pupils, staff and Old Girls. The Headmistress remarked that 'every name will bring back memories of days at St Bride's'. She was also made a life-member of The Guild, and it had been arranged for her to sit at a later date for a portrait by Greiffenhagen. Miss Renton later gifted this portrait to the School, and it hung in the School Hall in a surround designed by A.N. Paterson until the fire of February 1997, when it was safely rescued. It has since been restored and re-hung in St Bride's Hall, and although it perhaps gives today's pupils a misleadingly severe impression of St Bride's first and longest-serving Headteacher, who was by then 65 years of age, it is certainly true that were it not for Miss Renton, Lomond as it is today would not exist.

She was a woman who cared deeply about all of her pupils, regardless of their academic ability, and she always strove for the highest standards in all things. She never clung to outdated traditions merely for the sake of it, and education for her did not stop when the bell rang, for she believed that education involved the whole person. Her philosophy lives on in the Lomond School of today.

In summary, as M. McGregor, the School Captain, wrote in her tribute in *The Bridesian*, Miss Renton was a woman of:

> . . . kindness and sympathy; her understanding of human nature, her keen sense of justice and her appreciation of the funny side . . . her dislike of fulsomeness and exaggeration . . . has inspired every high ideal . . . .

Whoever succeeded Miss Renton as Headmistress of St Bride's was obviously going to find the task a difficult one, for as a former pupil who later became a member of staff commented, '. . . to past and present Bridesians, Miss Renton and St Bride's are one and the same'.

However, the task fell to Miss Mary C. Bell, who had for six years been Headmistress of St Margaret's School for Girls in Aberdeen. She had studied at Girton College, Cambridge, and had formerly taught in Manchester and Edinburgh. Miss Renton had, it seems, played a part in the selection of her successor, as she had on more than one occasion invited Miss Bell to the School. The Girls' School Company also had a new Chairman in Mr A. Peden Fyfe, who would serve until 1944.

MISS J. B. M. RENTON, L.L.A.
FIRST HEADMISTRESS OF ST BRIDE'S, 1895–1929.
A Gift to her on retiral from Past and Present Pupils
And by her presented to the School.

Miss Renton's portrait by Greiffenhagen.
The portrait still hangs in St Bride's Hall,
having been restored after suffering smoke-damage in the 1997 fire.

Part Two:

1930–1953 World War Two, The 'Victory Jubilee' and The Coronation

Miss Bell's First Decade at St Bride's

Perhaps predictably, at the end of her first year in charge Miss Bell commented that:

> During this year I have come to realise more and more what St Bride's meant to Miss Renton and what Miss Renton meant to St Bride's, and so to appreciate more and more her faith in entrusting the School to me.

On 10 January 1930, Miss Renton returned for the official unveiling of her portrait, in its Paterson surround. (Prior to its unveiling, the portrait had been exhibited at the Royal Academy in London.) Characteristically, Miss Renton had refused to be painted in academic dress, preferring a more informal effect, and Miss Bell commented at the unveiling that the portrait would serve as '. . . an inspiration to the girls of today, and the girls of the days to come'. Having summered in Switzerland and autumned in France, before sitting for the portrait in London during the winter, Miss Renton, who still had many years of life ahead of her, looked in splendid health.

Earlier in the Session there had been a half-holiday to mark the anniversary of the Armistice, when the School had been addressed by Lady Haig, wife of the late Earl Haig, whose engraving at that time hung in the Hall. A mumps' epidemic caused the cancellation of many events, but the Debating Society still managed to discuss the motion that 'Bald Men should Wear Wigs'. Five fish taken from the Burnbrae burn were presented to the new Headmistress, and in the summer, House Picnics were held at Loch Fyne, Crianlarich, and the Lake of Menteith. There were eight leavers from the Sixth Form (compared to today's fifty or more), six of whom went on

Miss M.C. Bell, Headmistress 1929–1943.

to Further or Higher Education of some kind, and the 'Renton University Scholarship' was awarded for the first time, the recipient being Rosemary Gordon. This Bursary had been set up by the Directors after consultation with Miss Renton, and annually awarded £25 per year for four years to a St Bride's pupil of three or more years standing who went on to University.

At Prize-Giving, Miss Bell commented, in remarks that would still be true of Lomond today, that:

> Schools (like) . . . St Bride's have much to be thankful for; they are not too big—they have not therefore to face the problem of the large class—they are able to devote themselves to the individual, so that it should be impossible for any girl to leave School without having been given a good chance to develop her own special gifts . . . and to realize their ideals.

The Burnbrae gardener, Roger, 1930.

In keeping with these ideas, one of the first topics to occupy the new Headmistress was that of marks and prizes. Miss Bell remarked that:

> Prizes . . . involve some system of marks, and marks in themselves can be dangerous. Children . . . begin to think that marks are more important than the lesson—and a commercial spirit must be banished from School.

As a consequence of Miss Bell's philosophy, ('. . . the average girl, no matter how hard-working, will never win a prize . . .'), marks were abolished altogether in the Preparatory Department, and were not given out until the end of term in the rest of the School. These alterations perhaps indicated a general relaxation of the School's regime, as Miss Bell believed in giving the girls freedom and responsibility wherever possible:

> I have rarely found that girls abuse freedom, and I have always found a great gain in the direction of responsible and reliable conduct when girls feel that they themselves are responsible and must discriminate for themselves.

Miss Renton's rule banning speaking in the cloakrooms after 8.50 a.m. was therefore abolished, as was the system of bad marks, as Miss Bell showed her belief in '. . . giving

Presentation of the prizes outside the Ardencaple Sports Pavilion, 1934.

the opportunity for self-control and self-discipline rather than the imposing of many rules'. The new Headmistress took care, however, not to dismantle too many of the traditions that Miss Renton had built up over 34 years:

> . . . the concern of the School (is) to educate the intellect, but more important still is the development of character . . . largely an unconscious process due to the acceptance by the girls of the School tradition. Miss Renton's great work was to build up a tradition . . . the greatest heritage that a school can possess.

In keeping with Miss Bell's philosophy of educating the whole person, 1931 saw the opening of the new playing-fields at Ardencaple on land leased from Mrs H. Macaulay Stromberg. Four blaes tennis-courts were provided, together with a blaes hockey-pitch, and a grass pitch (these facilities are of course still in use over 70 years later), whilst the School's pavilion was moved to Ardencaple from the Larchfield sports' field, after the St Bride's sports had been held there for the last time. At Prize-Giving, Miss Bell continued to expound her belief that schools should strive to cater for the entire range of ability:

> . . . all girls are not fit to go on with academic work . . . it is the duty of schools to provide an outlet for the girls who cannot pass examinations, but who possess excellent qualities of a different kind . . . . Schools in (Britain) have not yet solved the problem of the non-academic girls . . . nearly all can be fitted by education in the full sense of the word to be profitable members of a community and to contribute something to society.

Miss Bell also pointed out the great progress made by the Girls' Public Schools since their inception only 50 years or so before. They had built up:

1932 Dog Show at the rear of St Bride's.

. . . a fine public-school tradition organised on the model of the boys' Public Schools
. . . in this short time they have had to cover the ground covered by boys' schools in
centuries of evolution.

1932 saw an interesting range of leisure activities for the girls, including an Inter-House
Choral Competition (which ran in one form or another until the mid 1990s); a Dog Show
that attracted over 100 entries, (a bucket of cold water was apparently kept handy in case
of fighting); a boarders' cine-film show in the Hall, (Felix the Cat, Rin Tin Tin and Charlie
Chaplin were the stars); and a mock election which was easily won by the Conservative
candidate. (A rotten banana was thrown at the Labour candidate, in what was described
as a 'hostile atmosphere'!) The Debating Society discussed such motions as: 'Cats Should
Be Taxed'; 'Boys and Girls Should Have the Same Curriculum', (defeated by 30 votes to
6); 'It is Better to Live Next Door to a Bad Musician Than a Fried Fish Shop', (carried by 29
votes to 7); 'Modern Civilization is the Cause of World Unemployment', (carried by 16
votes to 14), and curiously, 'It is Dangerous for us to Sleep With The Moon Shining on Us',
(unanimously defeated).

Elsewhere in the School, Burnbrae become the proud owner of a new gramophone,
House Prefects' badges were introduced, Kathleen Adam toured America with the Scottish
Ladies' Hockey Team, new curtains were purchased for the stage from the proceeds of a
production of *A Winter's Tale,* and Kinnear House had a collection to 'send two poor children
for a fortnight to the seaside', whilst on their own House Picnic to Ardlui, '. . . it was very
exciting when something went wrong with the (taxi's) accelerator and it started buzzing'.
Meanwhile, Birkhall was sold after being in the School's ownership for only 16 years. At

Prize-Giving, Miss Bell, evidently possessing as much foresight as her predecessor, argued in favour of a 'gap year', suggesting that '. . . girls should not go to the university too young . . .', and advocating '. . . one year of post-matriculation education at home or abroad'. Prophetically too, she spoke of the wider world political situation, and commented that: '. . . we cannot regard the immediate future with complete equanimity'. World War Two was of course still seven years away, and in the meantime, Miss Bell was confident that St Bride's now possessed '. . . all that a school can reasonably require in the way of buildings, equipment and playing-fields'. Returning to her theme of the previous year, she added that:

> Character-training . . . is the goal of all school life—in work and play (to) make our
> girls broad-minded and tolerant, with a genuine admiration for truth and beauty. . . .
> We must create a free, healthy atmosphere (so that) . . . it is the accepted thing to be
> trustworthy and considerate, loyal and unselfish.

The Depression of the 1930s was beginning to bite, however, and the Government had recommended a cut in the salaries of state-school teachers. When this was implemented, the pay of teachers employed by the Girls' School Company was higher than that of state teachers. The result was a 5 per cent pay-cut in 1932 to bring Company and state salaries into line. (Dr Susan Milligan, in her book *Variety Without Disorder. A History of St Columba's School, 1897–1997*, published by St Columba's in 1998, notes that the cut in salary was restored by 2.5 per cent in 1937, and fully in 1939 for those staff who were five years from retirement age, so that pensions would not be affected.)

Also in 1932, the Girls' School Company changed its status from a share-holding Company to an Educational Trust, in order to gain exemption from income-tax.

Despite, or perhaps because of, the Depression, fees remained unchanged at between 40 and 45 guineas (£42 and £47.25) per term for boarders, depending on age. The Prospectus of the time gives an interesting insight into the flavour of the inter-war years; girls were still required to produce certificates (issued with their reports) at the start of each term stating that they had not had, or been exposed to, any infectious illness during the holidays, and Scarlet Fever and Diphtheria were clearly still a worry. At the Sanatorium (Kildare Lodge), a 'trained and experienced sister' was in charge, and 'extra trained assistance' was provided if an 'epidemic' occurred. Winter sports were lacrosse, hockey and netball; in the summer, tennis and cricket were played.

The Department of 'Domestic Science and Housewifery' continued to be a major selling-point of the School, over twenty years after its inception, offering girls as it did:

> . . . instruction in what pertains to the right ordering of a home as well as . . . cause
> them to regard the ordinary duties of home as worthy of the most serious attention,
> and will enable them to take up such duties in a competent and earnest manner.

The course, leading to the Higher Leaving Certificate, included training in 'Laundry, Sick-Nursing, High-Class Cookery and Advanced Needlework and Cutting Out.'

The boarding-houses were advertised as possessing 'airy and sunny' bedrooms, which were 'comfortably and daintily' furnished, whilst St Bride's itself featured 'well-lighted classrooms' and excellent 'heating, ventilation and drainage.' In the boarding environment, girls' health was 'carefully watched', and each House employed 'a lady experienced in all matters connected with health.' Hours of study were 'strictly limited' and 'any system of examinations involving over-pressure' was avoided, and 'every effort' was made 'to develop the taste of girls in music and reading, and to extend their general knowledge.' Indeed, so far as music was concerned:

> Gramophone lectures are arranged to cultivate knowledge of musical form and composition. The girls attend Subscription Concerts in town during the winter, when they have the opportunity of hearing the best trio and quartet parties and many of the famous musicians of the day.

The School's general aims, as stated in the Prospectus of this time and echoing Miss Bell's remarks at Prize-Giving, were, allowing for the differences in expression of the 1930s and seventy years later, perhaps little different from those highlighted by the current Headmaster, Mr Angus Macdonald:

> The highest importance is attached to the general training in character and in habits of order, as distinct from actual instruction, (whilst) . . . the obligations of mutual help and service which the School as a community imposes on all its members, are fully realised by older girls, who loyally accept responsibilities in connection with the happiness of the younger children and the general life of the School . . . .

Latin and Greek, together with drawing, painting and 'class singing' were on the syllabus, and the School provided an education to 'fit girls for the interests and responsibilities of social life'.

Interestingly, 1933 saw several 'skating holidays' during the Spring term, (those relaxed days long gone!), whilst the parquet floor which still exists in the Hall was laid. It was confidently proclaimed that '. . . splinters are now a thing of the past!'. (The floor was restored to perfect condition in December 1998.) The Debating Society discussed the motion: 'It is Better to Look a Greater Fool Than You Are, Than to be a Greater Fool Than You Look', and in Lansdowne at Hallowe'en, Miss Bell told ghost-stories by the light of turnip lanterns, whilst at Ashmount the girls roasted chestnuts and 'dooked' for apples.

In 1934, Armistice Day fell on a Saturday, and the two-minute silence was observed on the hockey-field. (The observance of the two-minute silence has been reintroduced on Armistice Day (11 November) within the last few years at Lomond.) Electric lights were installed at Lansdowne, and the Day Girls won the Hockey Cup 'in their new red girdles'. The Day Girls also sent 'a large collection of hand-knitted vests and woollies' to Glasgow. There was a plea for the School to build its own swimming-pool due to the 'inadequacy of the Shandon (Hydro) baths', but the recession was beginning to bite. Miss Bell commented at Prize-Giving on the tendency for parents to cut back on individual music tuition: 'In the stress of hard times it is a natural thing for parents to cut off the extras . . .' but she urged parents to '. . . pool their resources in the interests of the child . . .' and to 'provide the right conditions and environment for homework'. She also stressed once again that: 'The effort, sincerity and honesty put into work are far more important than prizes . . .', and with an obvious eye on the worsening international situation, drew a parallel between the government of a school and that of a country:

> . . . the creation of good feeling in a school . . . is as fundamental a necessity as it is in international relationships . . . Good feeling and behaviour will exist only where there is freedom for self-expression and for the development of personality under sympathetic guidance and without resentment of authority. In a free school, children are happy, natural and spontaneous and yet under . . . self-control.

Whilst it is doubtful whether Hitler was much impressed by Miss Bell's good advice, one Old Bridesian, who was living in Germany at the time, wrote that he had been sorely misjudged:

> I would seriously like to feel . . . that I could persuade people that 90 per cent of the atrocity propaganda which caused such horror in this country is utterly unfounded.

and also referred to the '. . . curious belief . . . that Hitler is something of an ogre'.

1935 saw a holiday for the Duke of Kent's wedding day, the girls eagerly listening to the event itself on the 'wireless', in a forerunner of the popularist Royal weddings of our own era. The Silver Jubilee of King George V fell in May, and St Bride's pupils received a 'long weekend' holiday to mark the occasion. A beacon chain was lit right across Britain, which Ruth Noble of S.6 hoped would be a 'symbol of an enduring peace in the world at large', whilst a walnut tree was planted at St Bride's to commemorate the Jubilee.

Remarkably for such a small school, by 1935, 21 St Bride's pupils were the children of 'Old Girls', and the annual Bridesian reunion was attended by over a hundred former pupils. Additionally, movement was again afoot on the property front, as Woodend in Millig Street, built in 1872, was purchased from Sir William Raeburn to be a Junior boarding-house, whilst Kildare Lodge, the Sanatorium in Colquhoun Street, was sold. Ashmount became the new 'San.', whilst Kinnear House was wired up for electric lighting as Burnbrae had been the previous year.

The School Sports were washed out, (new teak seats had been purchased for the fields by a subscription from the girls of 1929–35), but the Lansdowne boarders did manage a picnic at Loch Ard, taking advantage of the perfect weather and '. . . not arriving back till a quarter to nine'. Earlier in the session Lansdowne had debated the motion that 'The Nazi System . . . is a Menace to the Peace of Europe', which was carried by 11 votes to 6.

Meanwhile, at Prize-Giving, Miss Bell equally prophetically predicted that: 'The film and the wireless will perhaps become as important as the blackboard and the textbook.' and also that: '. . . in the near future, Biology and Social Science will find a place in every school.'

Woodend in Millig Street.

Senior Burnbrae girls outside the Loch Achray Hotel, 1934.

1st XI Hockey Colours.

2nd XII Lacrosse Colours.

Replica of Athletic Shield.

School Prefect's Badge.

Badge for Runner-Up of Athletic Shield.

School Captain's Badge.

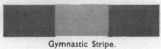

Gymnastic Stripe.

1st XII Lacrosse Colours.

2nd XI Hockey Colours.

1st VI Tennis Badge.

School Badges.

School Badges, 1935.

Video, Compact Disc and the Internet still lay fifty or sixty years ahead, however.

1936 was another eventful year in many respects. Miss Bell commented that the School had been 'victimised by infectious ailments', and there were frequent bouts of quarantine, particularly in the Preparatory Department, throughout the session.

There was also another holiday for the wedding of the Duke of Gloucester, which was celebrated at Kinnear House by a bonfire and fireworks' party, whilst the death of King George V was marked by a memorial service in St Columba's Church, and the girls all listened to the funeral service, the Prime Minister's speech and the Proclamation of the new King (Edward VII) on the radio.

On 24 March the *Queen Mary* was launched and sailed down the Clyde on its way to New York, with former pupil Janet Maxwell on board, whilst in April fourteen pupils visited Paris, hoping to meet 'some Russian princes'.

Tragedy struck the School in May 1936 when Alastair and John Robb, aged seven and five, were drowned whilst sailing their toy boat. (Alastair had attended St Bride's for three years, and his brother for one year.) In another aquatic accident the previous year, former pupil Evelyn Irons, who was then a journalist in London but who had previously lived at Ravenswood in Helensburgh and also at Shandon, saved her friend from drowning in the sea off the Cardigan coast. She received the Stanhope Medal from the Royal Humane Society in February 1936 for 'the bravest deed of the year', and was the first woman since Grace Darling in 1838 to whom the medal had been awarded. During World War Two, Miss Irons also became the first female war correspondent to be awarded the Croix de Guerre, which she received for her report on the capture of a Bavarian village by the French army. She also marched in triumph down the Champs Elysees at the liberation of Paris.

Evelyn Irons, 1936.
The first woman for almost one hundred years to be awarded the Stanhope Gold Medal by the Royal Humane Society for the 'Bravest Deed of the Year'.

Elsewhere, coinciding perhaps with the appointment of a 'Teacher of Diction', a Drama Club was established, whilst proposals were made for a new gymnasium. (These were not fulfilled for another 30 years.) Burnbrae girls held a 'melon picnic' in the summer term, whilst at Woodend the boarders were delighted by the beautiful gardens and stained-glass windows, and also to discover a 'spray' (shower) in the bathroom. Meanwhile at Ashmount, Miss Maris, who had been Housemistress for 15 years, retired and was presented with a 'portable wireless'. At Prize-Giving, Miss Bell remarked on parentally-condoned pupil absences, pointing out the extra work which this entailed for staff, and commenting that:

> . . . the repetition of work to one girl wastes the time of the class, and therefore trivial excuses for absence should not be made . . . . It is also important that girls should come back on the first day of term after holidays . . . .

Session 1936–37 marked the Silver Jubilee of *The Bridesian* magazine, whilst December 1936 saw the abdication of King Edward. The Coronation of King George VI in May 1937 was a time of great celebration all over Britain. At St Bride's, form-rooms were decorated with flags and bunting, whilst the Provost of Helensburgh distributed medals (which were given to each child), tins of chocolate and other souvenirs provided by the Town Council. A cherry tree with a commemorative plaque was planted at Burnbrae to mark the occasion, whilst Betty Campbell of S.6 was the Dunbartonshire Girl Guides' representative at the Imperial Coronation Camp near London. Coronation Day was described by pupils writing in *The Bridesian* magazine as:

> . . . a most stirring demonstration of the loyalty and affection of the people of the British Empire to the throne.

In this session too, the only other fire ever to strike St Bride's broke out in the kitchens and quickly sped to the Housekeeper's quarters above; (in 1997 these rooms comprised Lomond's Sixth-Year Centre). It was quickly extinguished, but not before the rooms had been badly damaged. A half-day holiday (Lomond lost no teaching time at all after the far more devastating fire of 1997) was granted as a result.

Meanwhile, Clarendon, (formerly named Torwood Villa) next to Ashmount in Millig Street had been purchased to replace Kinnear House (which was sold to a former pupil, Nancy Bonner [Mrs Campbell Wilson] and reopened as a private hotel), and opened in the autumn of 1937 as a Middle-School boarding-house. Clarendon had been built in the late 1880s and in the 1920s was the home of the Rickey family, who provided two School Duxes, (Elizabeth and Emily), and three Games Captains, (Emily, Jane and Kate), before it was sold to the Singer Sewing Machine Company. There were suggestions from Old Girls that Clarendon should be renamed Kinnear House to continue the name and tradition, but this idea never came to fruition.

1937 also saw the retirement of Cook/Housekeeper Annie Downs after 42 years' service to the School. 'Downs' who had had a longer association with the School than anyone, was presented with a wireless as a retirement gift.

Clarendon (c. 1950).

**'Annie' and Downs
outside St Bride's
c. 1913.**

In the Debating Society, the motions: 'Patriotism is an Outworn Tradition' (defeated by 26 votes to 12), and 'The More I See of Men, the More I Like My Dog', (defeated by 14 votes to 7), were discussed, and a proposal was put forward that a 'gramophone-record' library should be established. Miss Bell also introduced a system of marks for deportment, which would be counted towards the Form Gymnastics' Competition. She commented at Prize-Giving that:

> The general carriage of the School this term has been disappointing . . . . Personal pride should give every girl the desire to make the best of herself. It is as well to form a habit of good carriage while at school, as poor posture later in life may militate against success, as well as offending the aesthetic sense.

Miss Bell also called for pupils' homework to be unaided by parents. ('Homework is a necessity and should cause no over-pressure . . .'), and for more pupils to learn the piano and violin.

She recognised that 'two things that affect and influence the development of the modern child so strongly . . .', namely the wireless and the gramophone, militated against the mastering of an instrument, but felt that '. . .their importance must not be exaggerated'. Rather more accurately, and prophetically, a lecture by Mr Donald Grant on the European situation suggested that both Germany and Italy were 'expansive', and that both wanted to control Eastern Europe. Mr Grant stated that 'Fascism was going to cause disturbance . . .' and that it was '. . . bound to cause war sometime'.

By 1938, the rooms over the kitchens comprising bedrooms and a bathroom for the housekeeper, had been rebuilt and also provided space for the storage of drama costumes, but in October another fire occurred at Burnbrae, and the fire-brigade had to be called. In the spring, Mr R.G. Paterson, who had been a Director since 1901, and who was the brother of the architect A.N. Paterson, died. A picture painted by Alexander Paterson was presented to the School in memory of the Senior Director by his daughter. It depicts the Gateway to the Coliseum in Rome, and having fortunately survived the fire, hangs at present (2002) in the staffroom. Mr Paterson was quoted as being always '. . . sympathetic in supporting the ideal of progress in educational policy that has characterised the School from its earliest years'.

Meanwhile, girls attended lectures at the Victoria Halls on topics as diverse as The Bombay Mission Settlement; Summer and Winter Indian Trails; Modern Europe, and Conditions in Modern Russia, whilst the Literary and Debating Society argued the motions: 'Depicting Crime in Literature, on the Stage and on the Screen is Harmful', (defeated 26–11); and, rather innocently in view of what was to happen the following year: 'Dictators are More Trouble Than They are Worth', (carried unanimously). A staff play (there was another in 1994) entitled *Ambrose Applejohn's Adventure* was performed, and the party visiting Paris in April was reduced from 17 to 12 because of the need for quarantine due to illness; the 12 'survivors' witnessed serious rioting in Paris. Another party of S.6 pupils attended the Empire Exhibition in Bellahouston Park in May; this event had been formally opened by the new King and Queen (the late Queen Mother) at Ibrox Stadium. In addition, for the first time the School entered a team for the Schools' and Universities' Yacht Races at Clynder.

The Prize-Giving was attended by Miss Renton, and she doubtless approved of Miss Bell's announcement of the introduction of Music, Art and Domestic Science as subjects for the Leaving Certificate, (taken in S.6), as from 1940.

World War Two

The School Sports at Ardencaple in 1937 and 1939.

On 3 September 1939, War was declared by Britain on Germany and her allies, and during the winter term gas-masks were distributed in Helensburgh; St Bride's girls carried them everywhere they went, including their dormitories and classrooms. Air-raid practices followed some months later. However, Miss Bell was still able to comment that:

> The work and life of the School has been little affected by the international crisis. Helensburgh is regarded as a safe area to which children will be evacuated.

St Bride's' tradition of charitable help and service was put to good use, with the Sixth Form holding an auction in aid of the 'Refugee Fund' which raised £17.00, and other classes holding events such as spelling bees and sales of cakes and toffee. Woodend also donated to the 'Fresh-Air Fund For Cripple Children'.

Perhaps with the War in mind, the Literary and Debating Society discussed whether: 'The Invention of Flying is the Greatest Curse That Ever Befell Mankind'; the motion was unanimously defeated however.

The year was also notable for the fact that the Girls' School Company applied to the Government for Grant-Aided status; the application was for Park School initially, but was soon extended to cover St Bride's and St Columba's. Under the system, grants were made by the Government on the recommendation of Local Education Authorities, based on the loss made by a school in any one year, and the number of the school's pupils resident in the Local Authority area. One condition was that Local Authority representatives had to join the Board of Directors; another was that the grant could not be used to fund capital expenditure or loan repayments, and was only available to meet every-day running costs. Dr Milligan (*Variety Without Disorder*, op. cit.) notes that these restrictions meant that capital projects initiated by the Company in any of their three schools continued to be funded on a 'hand-to-mouth' one-off basis.

In 1940, somehow, under wartime conditions, funds were found for the outright purchase of the Ardencaple playing-fields, from J. Lawson and J. Hendry, whilst around 40 girls from The Park School were evacuated to Helensburgh, Clarendon being turned over to them. (The following year, Clarendon would be requisitioned by the Navy as a WRNS hostel.) Girls who had left St Bride's and gone elsewhere to board before the War also returned to the School, but because St Bride's had not been blacked out, evening activities during the months of early darkness, such as films, concerts, drama and debating, which were usually held in School, could not take place. Petrol-rationing curtailed the usual House picnics in the summer too, and Inter-House activities were affected, but apart from these fairly minor inconveniences, the session ran uninterrupted. There was, however,

1940: Burnbrae girls collect sphagnum moss in Glen Fruin for dressings for the wounded. They had done the same during World War One.

77

no Speech Day (Prize-Giving) on the usual scale; instead the girls met in the Hall on the last morning of term to hear the Prize-List read by Miss Bell. Meanwhile, at Burnbrae, at any rate, the girls had kept in touch with the progress of the War, since the Housemistress Miss King had had a wireless installed for this purpose. (Whilst listening to the wireless, the Burnbrae girls knitted 74 garments for the forces!)

By 1941, conditions had worsened somewhat (for instance, there was no heating in the dormitories), though once again the session ran uninterrupted. Black anti-splinter netting was placed over all windows, and there were regular air-raid practices; at Burnbrae, the library was converted into an air-raid shelter, whilst the girls 'dug for Victory', growing vegetables in the garden. Once again, evening social activities were curtailed during the winter, and they were therefore crammed into the short summer term, when the staff presented another play, this time *The Importance of Being Earnest*, and several other plays were also staged in aid of St Dunstan's.

Old clothes were sent to London to help victims of the Blitz, but when Clydebank was bombed by over 400 planes in March, (there were more raids in April and May), help was needed nearer home, and ten Rest Centres for the homeless were opened in Helensburgh. The only damage in Helensburgh itself appeared to be broken windows in the shops along Clyde Street, caused when a bomb fell on the beach, but in Clydebank, over 500 people were killed, and only 7 of the town's 12,000 tenements were undamaged. After the attack, the town's nocturnal population dropped from 50,000 to 2,000 overnight. In Helensburgh, church halls, two schools, and the Victoria Halls were pressed into action, and a Feeding Centre was established at The Granary. Greenock had also been hit, and the St Bride's girls watched in awe as the burning whisky, rum, sugar, molasses and oil turned the Clyde into a river of fire.

Elsewhere on the home front, Old Bridesian Miss Annie ('Nance') Anderson, (1889–1980), had been awarded the MBE for organising the Women's Voluntary Services for Civil Defence in West Dunbartonshire. Miss Anderson had attended St Bride's from Nursery to S.6, and also served as a member of staff, editing *The Bridesian* magazine for a time, establishing the Lennox Reading (1957) and Fruin Public Speaking prizes, and founding the 1st St Bride's Girl Guide Company in 1920. The Guide movement itself began in 1910, and *The Times*, on 21 May 1932, looked back at the spirit that had prompted its formation; it is clear that this philosophy dovetailed exactly with that of St Bride's and Miss Renton:

> At that time, over 20 years ago, women were just coming into their own in the work of the world. Character-development was actually more needed by them than by their brothers, since they had less opportunity of forming it in their comparatively secluded life. The needed it also in their capacity as mothers for imparting it to their offspring. The school education of girls had been put on a higher and steadily-improving footing ... but the problem of their character-training was as yet unsolved ....
>
> Now the girls were coming forward of their own volition to get the same adventure as their brothers. ... It was a big innovation.

The term 'Guides' was intended to give an idea of romance and adventure, while it indicated also their future responsibilities for directing their menfolk and bringing up their children on right lines. The general aim of its training was similar to that of the scouts—namely, to develop character and health and sense of service to others, while in particular it would give practical instruction in home-keeping and mothercraft . . . .

All are accepted in the sisterhood who can subscribe to our religious policy . . . namely love of God and love for one's neighbour . . . .

The Guides are . . . young women . . . who . . . are not content merely to fritter away their lives on inanities.

Nance Anderson was in addition a member of the Town Council and Helensburgh's first female magistrate. Her mother was also Annie Anderson (nee Templeton) of Drumgarve in John Street, which was gifted by the Andersons to the Burgh Council in 1946 for use as a Public Library; the house, which had been occupied by the Templetons for 76 years, lay empty for several years after the construction of a new Library on the site of St Bride's church in 1998, but is currently (2003) being converted into flats.

Back at School, there was no Speech Day, the girls gathering instead in the Hall to hear Miss Bell wish them a 'safe holiday'. This was no idle pleasantry, as France had fallen, and the two *Queens*, painted camouflage grey, were often to be seen in the Clyde, acting as troop-carriers.

By 1942, many Day-Girls had evacuees or members of the forces billeted with them; the War-effort went into overdrive, and a number of girls did farm-work or fruit-picking during the summer holidays. An impressive 156 lb. of rose-hips were collected by St Bride's girls to be made into syrup, and the proceeds of the sale were donated to the Prisoner of War Fund. The girls also collected 'unclaimed sheep's wool' from hedges and fences for the Women's Voluntary Service, whilst Burnbrae leavers presented apple trees instead of books; (the following year they presented currant bushes). Films shown during the session included *Salute to the Soviet* and *Ack-Ack*, (anti-aircraft). At the Closing Assembly in the Hall, which again replaced Prize-Giving, 'Motherland' and 'Song of Freedom' were sung. Miss Bell announced that the impressive sum of £323 4/1d (£323.20p) had been raised for various charities during the session, some of it by an auction sale at which bidding '. . . became very fierce at times, when eggs or a pot of jam or some other precious foodstuff was put up'.

The year was also notable for the fact that Old Bridesian Dr Nancy Miller of Netherton, Dumbarton, was awarded the MBE for her devotion to duty, and also the Lloyd's Medal for Bravery at Sea. Aged 26, she was the first woman to receive this medal. Dr Miller had been a surgeon on board the 9,000-ton Anchor Line vessel *Britannia* in the South Atlantic when it was shelled and sunk by the enemy. The order 'abandon ship' was given, but Dr Miller stayed at her post to help the wounded and dying. She remained until most of the ship's crew had been evacuated, and joined one of the last lifeboats to be launched. After 27 hours she was picked up by a small Spanish ship, which three days later was intercepted by a British ship. The survivors from the *Britannia* were taken aboard, where, strangely,

Dr Miller was reunited with her father who was surgeon on board. Forty-four people aboard another lifeboat died after 22 days adrift.

1943 saw the retirement of Miss Bell after 14 years in charge of St Bride's. To mark the occasion, the Directors presented a number of books to the Library in her honour, and the senior local Director, Sir Cecil Weir, commented in his tribute to the departing Headmistress that Miss Bell had been a 'leader of high intellectual quality and of strong and fearless character'. A picture presented in her memory hangs in today's staffroom (2003).

Despite the Headmistress's departure, the School's charitable work continued unabated, with a total of £289 12/5d (£289.62p) being raised during the session. One of the main events was a 'Mission Sale', which included a hoopla stall offering eggs as prizes. Four hens were also for sale, and were sold for 'a considerable sum'. The School contributed around £200 to Dunbartonshire's 'Wings For Victory' appeal, the target of which was £45,000 to pay for a Lancaster Bomber and Spitfire. Pupil entertainment included a mock trial in the Hall, in which an employee of a shipping company was accused of passing secret information to the enemy. The unfortunate person in the dock was found not guilty and was awarded the sum of £2,250 for defamation of character!

The new Headmistress was Miss M.N. Hensman, (M.A. Oxon.), who 'was acquainted with both (her) predecessors . . .' and had had '. . . the benefit of their friendship and advice'. Echoing Miss Bell's remarks of some years earlier, Miss Hensman commented during her first year that:

> Ever since I came to St Bride's I have been conscious that I have become the inheritor of a great tradition . . . . Tradition . . . can be inspirational if it is allied with progress.

Looking ahead to the School's Golden Jubilee in 1945, she added that there would be a 'great reunion' if the War had ended by then.

Miss Hensman soon introduced an innovative Citizenship Course for S.6 pupils, and in 1944, visits included a trip to College Street Special School in Dumbarton to see 'mentally deficient and physically deformed' children, and to the Helensburgh gas-works. Lectures were given to the group on the History of Helensburgh; Water Supply, and Careers (teaching, nursing and social work).

**Miss M.N. Hensman,
Headmistress 1943–1953.**

During the summer holidays, in a foretaste of today's Outward Bound Course for S.6, with echoes of Steinbeck's *The Grapes of Wrath*, eleven girls and two members of staff went berry-picking at Alyth in Perthshire. The party slept on wooden bunks in a hut with a corrugated-iron roof, rising at 6.30 a.m. to wash outside in cold water. The weight of berries picked was chalked on the hut door, whilst in the evenings the Headmaster of the local school invited the girls to listen to his wireless. By the end of their stay the girls had more than covered their expenses, donating £13 6/6d, (£13.32p) to The Merchant Seamen's Association. Earlier in the session, eggs had again been raffled at the Mission Sale, along with 'many other attractive articles', whilst a 'threepenny bit' (a coin worth about a penny) collection at Burnbrae raised £35 for St Dunstan's. A carol service, the first since the start of the war, was held in the Hall. Meanwhile at Woodend, the girls had to perform household duties 'owing to the shortage of domestic staff', and at Lansdowne, in between 'fire-parties' for training purposes in case of an incendiary attack, the girls adopted a black cat which promptly produced three kittens, 'two of which we had to drown'.

Sadly, during the year, Mr Peden Fyfe, Chairman of The Girls' School Company for 15 years, died. He was succeeded by Mr Norman Millar. In 1945, at St Bride's, two long-serving members of staff retired. Miss Renton's sister, Lizzie, (she was always known as 'Miss Lizzie' to distinguish her from the Headmistress), retired after over 40 years' service as a visiting teacher of the piano and violin, whilst Miss Jack, who taught French and was Second Mistress, retired after 31 years at St Bride's.

The 'Victory Jubilee'

In fact, although the year 1945 marked the official Golden Jubilee of the School's foundation, it was decided to delay the celebrations until the following year, when catering and travel conditions might have improved. To mark the occasion, it was decided to launch an Appeal to help build the 'Victory Jubilee Extension', which would provide new sports' facilities extending from the present Music Studio (Ardenlee's old coach-house) on the line of the present gymnasium towards Millig Street, extending right out to the John Street wall, where the changing rooms were to be. The complex would provide a gymnasium/badminton/assembly hall, a squash-court and a 50' x 26' swimming-pool. The estimated cost was £10,500 (or £8,500 without the squash court). An Appeal was launched to raise £2,000, the sum to be split between the fund-raising efforts of the Guild on the one hand and the School on the other. The plans, and a model of the proposed extension, designed by Mr G.W. Clissold, one of the Directors of St Bride's, were displayed at the Guild AGM. Life-Membership of the sports' facilities would be granted to anyone contributing £10.00 or more to the Appeal, whilst all others, including pupils, (perhaps rather controversially), would be charged for using them. The existing gymnasium, (the present Music Studio) was to be turned into a Biology laboratory, with a floor-level 3 feet higher than the hall; a gap of 22 feet in its wall would open into the new sports' hall, so that it could be used as a platform for functions. These facilities would, it was felt, make St Bride's 'one of the most up-to-date schools in the UK'. A brochure, drawn up by Sir Cecil Weir, was sent out

**Artist's impression (drawn by Miss Mary Allan of the Old Girl's Guild)
of the proposed Sports' Hall, from the plans of Mr G.W. Clissold, Director,
and Chairman of the Jubilee Fund Committee.**

to the Guild members in December, and notice of the Jubilee was also printed in *The Glasgow Herald* and *The Scotsman*.

Elsewhere in the School's affairs, only 58 girls managed to attend School on one day in January, due to a heavy snow-fall, whilst in the same month the first S.6 Burns' Night was held; this is still an annual event at Lomond.

In February, pupils had their first 'wireless lesson' after a radio had been presented to the School, whilst on 8 May great celebrations occurred on VE (Victory in Europe) Day, which was of course a School holiday. Ships in the Clyde sounded their hooters, searchlights were on and rockets and flares were fired. The girls were able to listen to Prime Minister Winston Churchill's speech on their new radio. Subsequently, 'real oranges' appeared at the Mission Sale!

In celebratory mood, the School held a mock election (there had been a coalition government during the War), and with no staff present, '. . . continued heckling added greatly to the atmosphere'. The Labour candidate claimed to have been down the mines from the age of 8, and there was also a Communist candidate, on the appearance of whom, '. . . the derisive booing grew even more deafening'. The audience became '. . . riotous and the Chairman's bell quite inaudible' until the voting took place. The Conservative candidate was elected by 6 votes (nationally, there was a Labour 'landslide', not unlike that of 2001), and the candidates appeared on the balcony to receive their acclaim.

1946 can be summed up in two words: 'The Jubilee'. The year got off to a good start when Clarendon was returned to the School after 5 years as a hostel for WRNS. Plans of the proposed sporting facilities were exhibited in the School, and it was hoped that these would '. . . make St Bride's an even brighter star in the educational firmament'.

On 1 June there was a reception in the Victoria Halls (the Government's official V.E. Day celebrations were held on 8 June) and speeches were given by, amongst others, the Provost of Helensburgh and the Chairman of The Girls' School Company. Provost Lever interestingly remarked that:

> The School is a great factor in bringing families to Helensburgh, though it is partly to blame for the high cost of houses in the town. . . . The town and the School are so closely allied that progress in the School means progress in the town.

Meanwhile, Mr D. Stewart, Convenor of Dunbartonshire Council, spoke of '. . . the spirit of friendship. . . so noticeable between pupils and teachers . . .', and, in a spirit of co-operation between the state and private sectors that is perhaps not so noticeable today, remarked that:

> St Bride's occupies a very important place in the education system of the County as it has facilities lacking in the County schools and can give education from infancy to university standard.

From the Victoria Halls, those assembled (including 160 'Old Girls') moved on to St Bride's to witness the laying of the foundation stone of the new development by Miss Renton, 17 years after her retirement; (Miss Bell was also present.) £2,200 had already been raised towards the cost of the new buildings. The stone, which still exists in its original position at the rear of the present Music Studio (2003), is hollow and contains a sealed canister which encloses some coins, copies of the Jubilee literature and a copy of the current edition of *The Helensburgh and Gareloch Times*. In a short speech, Miss Renton reminded those present that she had been warned by the Rev. Prof. Lindsay, Chairman of the Directors in 1895, when Helensburgh High School was founded, that the Girls' School Company was '. . . thrusting itself into Helensburgh, uninvited, unsupported, without any certainty of a welcome'. In fact, a parent in those early days had later confided to Miss Renton that at first the locals were '. . . suspicious of their high-faluting ideas'.

On the following day, 2 June, a Jubilee Thanksgiving Service was held in St Bride's Church. The Very Reverend Charles L. Warr commented that:

> One man soweth, and another reapeth. At the very heart of this commemoration service is the moving recollection of those who have gone before us, who loved this School and served it, and bequeathed it to us as a precious heritage.

On the Monday, 3 June, the Directors treated the entire senior school to a visit to the Tower Cinema, where the girls, who occupied the whole balcony, saw *Rhapsody in Blue*. Afterwards they consumed 'Jubilee cakes' (one of which bore 50 candles) in the Hall, having been joined by the Kindergarten, who had been having a 'picture show' of Mickey Mouse films.

The laying of the foundation stone for the proposed new Sports' Hall by Miss J.B.M. Renton, 1 June 1946.

St. Bride's School, Helensburgh
Jubilee 1895 - 1945

The Headmistress and Directors
have pleasure in inviting

to the following functions :-

On Saturday Afternoon, June 1st, 1946, at 2-30 p.m., in the Victoria Hall — a Reception followed by Tea in the School.

On Sunday Afternoon, June 2nd, 1946, at 3 p.m., in St. Bride's Church — a Service of Thanksgiving.

(Preacher: The Very Rev. Charles Warr, C.V.O., D.D., L.L.D., Dean of the Thistle, St. Giles' Cathedral, Edinburgh).

R.S.V.P. to the Headmistress by Saturday, May 11th, 1946.

An invitation to the Jubilee Reception in the Victoria Halls and to the Thanksgiving Service in St Bride's Church, 1 and 2 June 1946.

Miss Hensman and others then planted the Jubilee Tree, a flowering cherry, to the accompaniment of a Latin incantation read by the School Captain, Jean Bruce. The tree, at the inner corner of the East Wing, was fortunate to survive the fire of 1997, which raged only a few yards away, but was removed to make way for the new building.

A number of girls who had been evacuated to 'The Dominions' at the start of the War now returned to St Bride's, whilst in *The Bridesian* magazine, a former pupil wrote that:

> St Bride's . . . has created, maintained and developed her traditions during one of the greatest upheavals in human history . . . . St Bride's has lived through no ordinary half-century, but one which has seen the passing of one era and the birth-pangs of another.

Elsewhere in the life of the School, a half-holiday was granted in honour of Gilda Robert's Scholarship to Oxford; the Annual Sale raised £292, and the Debating Society discussed the motion: 'The Allies Ought Not To Have Used the Atomic Bomb', (which was defeated). An S.6 Citizenship Course was held in the summer term; the Day Girls' House was abolished, and there was a small fire at Lansdowne. Burnbrae held their first picnic since before the War, visiting Glen Douglas, and over 100 'Old Girls' submitted their news to the magazine. (Membership of the Guild stood at a staggering 700.)

At the Prize-Giving, at which the prizes were presented by Nance Anderson, MBE, The Very Reverend Charles Warr reminded the girls that: 'In the difficult years that lie ahead, your country will depend greatly on the character of its womanhood.' He also referred to '. . . the struggle between the materialistic and the spiritual conceptions of human life', and urged schools to stress citizenship and moral and spiritual development, since 'knowledge and ability' were not enough:

> People do not deserve your respect just because of what they have, but only because of what they are, in character and in personality.

He stressed that '. . . life is given . . . by God as a sphere for service . . .', and urged those present to remember '. . . the consecrated service and unselfish endeavour that were so freely given towards the expansion and development of St Bride's by those who are now at rest.'

The Post-War Years

The following year, 1947, saw the retirement of Miss King after 28 years, during which she had been Senior English Mistress, Sixth Form Mistress, Burnbrae Housemistress, and Editor of *The Bridesian* magazine. She was presented with a Sheraton tea-caddy, a wireless and a cheque, and in turn gifted an 'antique silver cup' to the School for 'speech-work'. (This cup was discovered at Larchfield in the summer of 1998, and was presented to the winner of the Senior Lennox Reading Competition at Prize-Giving in June 1998. It is hoped that it will once again be presented annually.)

During 1947, Lansdowne had abandoned its 'unpopular crocodile walks' on Saturdays in favour of cycle-rides; Clarendon held a pageant on the front lawn, depicting historical scenes from the Romans to The Great War, and S.6 had a talk from a former suffragette on 'Women's Struggle For Independence'. A Careers' lecture advised the girls not to become 'a hostess on an airliner' because the 'glamour ended with the uniform', and also suggested that it was 'a great pity that only the "duds" of a class specialised in Domestic Science', since the subject was both 'interesting and profitable'. Another lecture by Captain Escott North, complete with cowboy outfit and pistol, on the subject 'Cowboys and Cattlemen', ended with the lassoing of a pupil, whilst the Debating Society discussed the motion that: 'Certain Films, The Press, and Crime Stories Are Responsible For the Increase in Crime', which was defeated.

The School roll now stood at 260, which was an increase of nearly 40 since the reopening of Clarendon as a Middle-School house in 1946. Forty-one girls passed the Higher Leaving Certificate, and 49 former pupils were at university, including four at Cambridge and one at Oxford. Eight girls were training to be doctors. The Appeal continued, with Mr Blackie, Director of The Company, suggesting that donations of antique furniture could be made for auction in aid of the Fund. The first formal Speech-Day since the start of the War was held in the Victoria Halls, and in November, the entire School listened to the wedding of Princess Elizabeth.

1948 was marked by the death at the age of 81 of James Brennan, who had been a gardener at Lansdowne Park for over 50 years. The first whole-School photo since the start of the War was taken, and a day's holiday was given to celebrate the Silver Wedding Anniversary of the King and Queen, (the late Queen Mother). The Dramatic Society presented four one-act plays; a Hallowe'en fancy-dress party was held in the Hall, and Captain Lawson, a 'master-diver', who was assisted into his 'complicated diving-suit' by three pupils, gave a lecture to S.6. A lecture on post-war Germany was also given during the session.

Mr Blackie's suggestion of the previous year had obviously borne fruit, since a sale of furniture and household effects was held in Lindsay's Auction Rooms in aid of the Jubilee Fund, whilst a 'Shakespeare Afternoon', when various scenes from the plays were read, was held to celebrate the Bard's birthday. A dog-show was also held, and 'barks in every key' sounded across the field. At Speech-Day (this title seems to have been preferred at this time to 'Prize-Giving'), which was attended by Miss Renton, it was reported that the roll now stood at 270. There was also a waiting-list, and a number of girls had had to be refused admission. New accommodation was obviously needed, but an increase in projected costs, and Government post-war restrictions, had prevented a start to the new facilities.

Meanwhile, mid-day meals for the 55 girls who travelled to School from outside the town were being supplied by the 'Helensburgh Food Centre', and a Cadet Unit of the Red Cross had been formed in School. Miss Hensman made a plea for parents to allow their daughters to remain for a sixth year, to 'achieve a poise and maturity they lacked before . . .', whilst prizes were awarded on a non-competitive basis; all achieving 75 per cent (or 65 per cent in S.6) received one.

By 1949 the new National Health Service meant that contributions to the Strathblane Cot were no longer required. Meanwhile, after a three-year break, the Day Girls' House was resurrected in the hope that it would have a 'psychological effect on the spirit of enthusiasm and unity so sadly lacking at present . . .'; a Festival of Music and Verse-Speaking was also held for the first time, whilst significantly, the girls were interested, when attending a concert given by the Halle Orchestra, that there were 'so many women in the orchestra'. A half-holiday was granted in June to mark Katherine Donald's award of a bursary to Edinburgh University, whilst former pupil Jenny Young became the first woman to be elected to the Girls' School Company's Board of Directors.

Elsewhere, a joint debate with Hermitage School argued the case that 'The Day-School System Gives A Better Education Than The Boarding School' (carried), whilst S.6 heard lectures on both missionary work in China and astronomy, and visited shipyards in Port Glasgow; Glasgow University Observatory, and a school for 'backward children' near Bowling that contained some 'ineducables'.

In the summer, the girls swam 'in somewhat arctic conditions' in Helensburgh's open-air pool; the Clarendon boarders 'thoroughly enjoyed' their tennis, 'except for the midges', whilst the Lansdowne girls went on a picnic to the Ayrshire coast on a state-of-the-art coach 'complete with radio'.

In 1950, the roll stood at 276, and Miss Hensman spoke of the need for further accommodation being a 'desperate problem'. Sir Cecil Weir, Honorary President of the Girls' School Company, suggested that it would 'soon be possible' to build. Lansdowne celebrated its 25th Anniversary as a boarding-house, whilst in an Inter-House Drama Competition, the Day Girls staged a scene from *The Pageant of Anne Boleyn* in which St George wore chain-mail 'evolved from dyed dishcloth yarn'.

1951 saw the retirement of Miss Crawford, Head of Music, who had been at St Bride's for thirty years, whilst several other members of staff suffered serious illness. Lt. Colonel Barge, one of the Company's local Directors, referred again to the need for new buildings in light of the increased roll, and commented that: 'Finance and the necessity for permits . . . stood in the way . . . but classrooms must come first . . .'.Once again, the need for 'permits' echoed 1997's planning permission delay with the new school.

Miss Hensman again expressed disappointment that some St Bride's pupils were sent to other boarding-schools for a sixth year, and referred to the 'diversity of careers' taken up by St Bride's own S.6 leavers.

Swimmers at Helensburgh's open-air pool.

Tree planting in Glasgow Street, Coronation year.

The planting of the Coronation tree by the East Wing, 1953.

Meanwhile, S.6 pupils visited John Brown's Shipyard to attend the launch of the oil-tanker *Clydewater*, and an appeal was made for 'Biblewomen' to join the Punjab Mission.

Prizes were still being awarded for perseverance, as well as for intellect, and at Prize-Giving in June, The Hon. Victoria Bruce, Governor of Duke Street Prison in Glasgow, commented on the 'similarity between life in school and life in prison'. She also commented on the importance of imagination, which allowed one to 'put oneself in the other fellow's place', and suggested that a lack of it produced the selfishness which was 'the root cause of most of the ills of modern society'.

1952 was notable for the death of King George VI. Two minutes' silence was observed, and a Memorial Service was held in St Columba's Church. The girls listened to the actual funeral service on the 'wireless'.

In this year too, the School Orchestra was formed, and the first School Caretaker was appointed. A mock election was won by the Conservatives, and the first joint debate was held with Keil School, the motion being that 'The Education of Women Is As Undesirable As It Is Unnecessary'. The motion was defeated by 44 votes to 11, *The Bridesian* magazine reporting that the girls' votes were supported by 'the more egalitarian of the visitors'.

S.6 pupils visited Broadcasting House, Birrell's Sweet Factory at Anniesland and Dumbarton Sheriff Court, where the cases heard included one involving the pollution of sausages. Sixteen girls also visited Amecy in France, and the Dramatic Society staged *Two Gentlemen of Verona*, the proceeds going to improve stage lighting.

1953 was a year of great change, both in St Bride's and in the wider world beyond. Miss Renton passed away on 12 February, aged 89. A Memorial Service was held in St Columba's. *The Helensburgh and Gareloch Times* quoted Sir Cecil Weir, who said that those who were Miss Renton's pupils would remember her '. . . as a firm and kindly personality, a gracious and warm-hearted lady, and a highly-talented and intelligent Headmistress'.

This year also saw the departure of Miss Hensman, who left to become a novice Anglican nun. (Sister Mary Frideswide wrote to Mr Macdonald, Headmaster of Lomond, in 1998, to express her condolences after the fire. She died in 2001.) Miss Hensman, who had been Headmistress at St Bride's for ten years, urged her pupils to see her departure not as '. . . a renunciation, but as a joyous adventure for God'. She was presented with a radiogram by the School, and with records by the Guild, but she in turn returned her gifts to the School in the hope that when the girls used the radiogram they would think of her.

The Coronation of Queen Elizabeth II was commemorated by the planting of 57 trees in Glasgow Street by girls from the Upper School as part of Helensburgh's programme of celebration. The School had three days' holiday to mark the occasion. All the girls received mugs and tins of sweets from the Town Council, and a commemorative tree (a pyrus) was planted in front of the East Wing. (This tree too disappeared to make way for the new building in 1998.)

The new Headmistress was Miss Rachel Drever Smith, whose nephew, David, then an M.P., who had been a pupil at St Bride's in 1914 at the age of five, presented the prizes in June. He advised the girls in his speech that 'TV should be treated with discretion'. Miss Drever Smith's father had been Headmaster of Inverness Royal Academy and President of the Educational Institute of Scotland. She had previously been Headmistress and Classics

**Miss Rachel Drever Smith,
Headmistress of St Bride's, 1953–1972.**

teacher at Sherborne School in Dorset.

By now, the sum raised towards the new building was £3,200, but due to increasing costs and to the difficulty of obtaining planning permission, plans for the Sports' Hall and swimming-pool had regrettably to be dropped. New plans had in fact been drawn up to add two much-needed classrooms to the East Wing, and it was stated that '. . . the long hoped-for building extensions are about to become matters of fact'. (The completed rooms are in 2001 the two biology laboratories.)

Elsewhere in the School's affairs, the first official Swimming Gala for the schools of the area was held at Helensburgh's outdoor pool, and an S.6 Variety Show included the 'Burnbrae Can-Can'.

Part Three:

St Bride's School—
The Last Two Decades

In 1954 the Guild presented a desk, chest of drawers and a chair to the Headmistress's study in memory of Miss Renton. (These lovely items of antique furniture were unfortunately destroyed in the 1997 fire.) A 'book-trough' was also presented in Miss Renton's memory to the Library by the London Group of the Guild.

The roll now stood at 297, and it was decided that the new addition to the East Wing would house the Kindergarten and forms 1 and 2. There were also plans for a new Art Room, but it was felt that space would limit any further expansion.

On the wider front, Sir John Hunt and Sir Edmund Hilary, who had climbed Mount

The chestnut tree that stood to the east of St Bride's before the construction, in 1954, of the classrooms that now form the Biology Laboratories.

Everest the previous year, gave a lecture in Glasgow which was attended by four pupils of the School, whilst the entire Senior School attended a showing of *The Ascent of Everest* at Helensburgh's Tower Picture House.

1955 saw the retiral of Miss Emlyn, after 27 years of teaching History, in the year that women teachers finally gained salary equality with males in the profession. Miss Emlyn also ran the Library, which at this time had a stock of around 1,300 books, and she had just introduced the Dewey Decimal system of cataloguing. At another mock election in May, the Conservatives were again victorious, beating the SNP into second place. S.6 received a lecture on 'How To Become an M.P.' given by Mr J. Johnston, whilst at the Lansdowne Guy Fawkes and Hallowe'en party, 'the greatest thrill of the evening was a lighted taper falling into a boxful of bangers and barking doggies'. The Lansdowne Christmas party was fortunately spared any unscheduled pyrotechnics; in fact '. . . the greatest fun was a team game in which members of staff as well as girls had to eat a water-biscuit at top speed'.

Before Lansdowne could fully enjoy its new water-main, laid during the year, Helensburgh experienced a water-shortage in September, and only S.6 boarders were allowed to join the day-girls back at School. A two-hour lunch-break was established to allow pupils to go home to eat; this afterwards led to the permanent adoption of a one and a half-hour lunch-break, (compared to the present fifty-five minutes on Mondays and Fridays and one hour five minutes on other days). Other boarders were off School for two weeks, and the shortage was such that, unbelievably in 2002, 'every shower of rain was welcomed'. The year also saw Mr J. Tindall succeed Mr Millar as Chairman of the Girls' School Company.

Fees in 1956 were £95–£100 per term for day-girls, and £112–£117 per term for boarders. These sums included all books and stationery, but not laundry or sewing-materials. To raise additional funds, part of Ashmount's garden was sold for building. Miss Drever Smith, speaking at Speech Day, stated that of the girls who had passed the Leaving Certificate during the previous seven years, 30 per cent had gone on to university, and only 5 per cent had not gone on to further education of some kind. Gwyneth Guthrie (whose picture appeared in the 1997 post-fire Appeal Brochure) had gained a Diploma at Glasgow School of Dramatic Art and the James Bridie Medal. The Headmistress stressed, however, that over and above examination results, the 'really important thing is the amount of honest, single-minded endeavour that goes into the work'. Also at Speech Day, Sir James Robertson, OBE, Head of Aberdeen Grammar School, commended the opportunities that were available in the 'Colonial Territories', and prophetically stated that '. . . whatever happens in Africa in the next fifty years will react on the future of the world'. He also went on to add that 'what happens in Africa will be determined by the . . . service given . . . by the English-speaking races'.

In 1957, Miss Drever Smith stated at Prize-Giving that:

The continued growth of the School and the increasing demand for places . . . are becoming, because of the inadequacies of our present accommodation, an embarrassment. I think of St Bride's as a neighbourhood school, and I dislike having to refuse admission to the children of my neighbours.

She felt that classes were becoming too large, and too mixed in ability. The introduction of 'O' grades in 1960 would involve a 'radical revaluation' of St Bride's syllabi, and if a broad curriculum was to be adequately staffed, then the roll had to be maintained or even increased. Consequently, the Headmistress stated that '. . . the Directors have agreed that we should envisage the gradual development of a two-stream School'. There was still the problem, however, of accommodation; with echoes of 1998, the Headmistress commented:

> Further building on the existing site would have much reduced our space, already inadequate, for play, and would, I fear, have still further stretched the admirable patience of our neighbours.

Consequently, the Preparatory Department was to move from St Bride's to Ashmount, which was currently operating as the Sanatorium, and the 'San' was to be rehoused in a 'small, modern and more labour-saving building' which was under construction. The move would free five classrooms in St Bride's (2002's English rooms and Biology laboratories), for use by the Senior School.

Also at Prize-Giving, Mr Anderson, CBE, formerly Chief Inspector of Schools for Western Scotland, reminded those present that teachers did not just teach subjects, but 'human beings', and emphasised the importance of parental co-operation: 'There should be no conflict . . . between . . . standards of hard work (at) school . . . and at home.' Mr Anderson also reminded the girls of their obligations:

> We should try to pay the rent for our room in the world, and the better the room, the higher the rent . . . . (St Bride's girls) should pay back to the people with no advantages something of what they themselves had received.

In keeping with this precept, pocket-money donations had raised £35 to support a Hungarian refugee child. Meanwhile, Burnbrae girls had purchased a 'four-speed gramophone' at a cost of £20.00, the sum being raised by a coffee-morning, and on 1 April, the Lansdowne girls appeared for breakfast in their pyjamas and dressing-gowns. Despite the fact that they had their clothes on underneath their night attire, this behaviour was obviously considered to be the height of decadence! The House-Mistresses remained so unperturbed, however, that the girls vowed to do it again in the future.

At Woodend there were four budgies, named Nasser, Joan of Arc, Helen of Troy and Florence Nightingale, but 'unfortunately Smokey the cat is always killing birds, so we have a lot of funerals'. There were also two married ladies on the staff, apparently the first in the School's history, whilst a lecture on the possibilities of space-travel by the Professor of Astronomy at Glasgow University left the girls 'rather less optimistic about reaching the Moon in our own lifetime' than they had previously been. The Professor hoped that '. . . our grandchildren or great-grandchildren would master . . . space-travel'. In fact, the first landing on the Moon was only a few years away.

Burnbrae before the fire with its original (1859) roof.

Burnbrae in 2002, with the mansard roof constructed in 1958.

The Burnbrae Fire

1958 was notable for the most serious fire to strike one of the School's properties until that of 1997. Fire broke out at Burnbrae between one and two a.m. on the night of Friday, 21 February (the 1997 fire occurred on 27 February). Co-incidentally, just as Mr Macdonald was absent from the School (in Germany) on the night of the 1997 fire, so Miss Drever Smith was in Aberdeen, attending a meeting of the Guild's Aberdeen Group. Many of the Headmistress's remarks about the Burnbrae fire were also applicable 39 years later:

This has been a horrifying experience and none of us is likely to forget it in a hurry . . . providentially, the legends that will grow . . . will be untainted by tragedy.

Miss Drever Smith thanked the fire-brigade, local contractors and all connected with the School:

. . . who have steadfastly kept things running more normally than I could have believed throughout all the disruptions and anxiety. I cannot begin to tell you of all they have done . . . with good humour, determination and judgement . . . .

The Burnbrae girls were evacuated to Ashmount and Lansdowne: 'What a sight we must have been in pyjamas and dressing-gowns, with our hair in pins . . .', and were subsequently sent home for the weekend. They returned to lodge with day-girls or to be squeezed into one of the other Houses. Despite the destruction of the whole attic floor at Burnbrae, the evacuation was carried out so smoothly that the Headmistress was able to comment:

It is a great thing to see good training . . . organisation (and) discipline . . . stand the test . . . . What was done at Burnbrae on the night of the fire remains as an example to us all.

Most of the House was still standing, and sausages rescued from the oven later in the morning were 'borne in triumph down to Clarendon for the Burnbrae breakfast'. Miss Drever-Smith was shocked, however, by the 'wholesale and systematic destruction that of necessity had to follow the fire, as 'walls, roofs, floors, ceilings, and the staircase fell before the onslaught'. (Unfortunately, the sitting-room had just been redecorated.) However, '. . . the Phoenix . . .' (which was to be a symbol of the new Lomond in 1998) 'was obviously going to rise improved, enlarged and altogether the better for the holocaust . . .'. Burnbrae was rebuilt with the mansard roof that still existed until demolition in 2002, whilst normal routine in School was scarcely disturbed, despite the fact that as in 1997:

. . . the wreckage, the smells of charred wood and sodden plaster, and the thought of the work and planning ahead were enough to make anyone feel that a return to normal would be a long time ahead.

During the summer holidays of 1958, Miss Drever Smith watched with 'anxiety and with mounting hopes' as the rebuilding progressed. Importantly, the reallocation of buildings depended on Burnbrae being open at the start of session 1958–59. On the morning after the fire, a few months previously, the contractors had promised the Headmistress, as she stood amongst the blackened and sodden ruins, that they would 'make it better . . . than it ever was', and true to their word, as in the summer of 1998, during the last week of the holidays there were 19 workmen, including:

> . . . blacksmiths, joiners, plasterers, painters, electricians, all putting finishing touches, (whilst) the teaching staff returned in a body a week before School opened and embarked with zeal and resource upon tasks which do not, even in these days, usually form part of (their) professional lives. They swept and scrubbed, they cleaned and polished . . . and emerged, because of intelligent and happy teamwork, unscathed.

By the start of the Autumn term, Burnbrae had been completely redecorated, and the top floor totally renovated, with two large dormitories created where there had previously been four small ones.

*　　*　　*　　*

Elsewhere in the life of the School, a 'Gramophone Record Club' met on Saturday mornings to play Louis Armstrong and Chris Barber records; the prefects, who now had their own study, formed a 'skiffle group', and performed a 'very amateurish calypso' at the Lansdowne Hallowe'en Party, whilst the Debating Society discussed the motions: 'We Should Have Been Better Off Without the Discovery of Petrol', and 'Women Should Not Use Cosmetics'.

Concern was also expressed at the rising costs of producing *The Bridesian* magazine; (a decade later it would cease publication). Meanwhile, 'Old Girl' Jenny Young was elected Helensburgh's first female Provost, whilst Miss Ness retired after 30 years of teaching Music.

At Speech Day, Mr W. Blackie, Chairman of the local Directors, informed those present that it had finally been decided that funds were insufficient to carry out the Victory Jubilee plans. The two new classrooms had cost over £6,000, some of which had been provided by the Girls' School Company. He commented that:

> The Board . . . hope that the time will come when all the aims and hopes of 1945 have been fulfilled, but the School is not endowed, and capital improvements can only be carried out by instalments.

However, independent schools were now allowed to apply for Direct Grant status, and the Company's three schools were accepted into the system the following year.

Meanwhile it had also been decided to relocate the Preparatory Department to

Clarendon, rather than to Ashmount, since the latter building had proved so suitable as a Junior boarding-house. There would in the future be no Middle School House; Juniors would either be in Woodend or Ashmount, and Seniors in either Lansdowne or Burnbrae. Thus only one move of House would be required in each girl's School career. The Senior houses would take girls from 12 years of age upwards. Meanwhile the new sanatorium was being built in Burnbrae's grounds, and Miss Drever Smith reiterated her aim of establishing two streams in each year-group, (the policy readopted in theory, although not actually for very long in practice, by Lomond in 1996, after a roll of over 550 had produced three classes in each year-group for a time), enabling setting to take place on a subject-by-subject basis. The School also underwent a full two-week inspection by HMIs.

By 1959, the Preparatory Department had moved to Clarendon, and a 'runner' (a prefect with a black brief-case) was dispatched with mail and messages from St Bride's every morning. The move had freed five extra classrooms in St Bride's, created more playground space, and enabled 'setting' in most subjects to become the norm. It was the Headmistress's hope that this would allow 'the more rapid advancement of abler girls', their earlier presentation for the Leaving Certificate, and consequently a spare session for more advanced work, although '. . . to meet within the framework of the smaller school all the needs of our pupils is a difficult aim'. Meanwhile, at Clarendon, the juniors had established '. . . many a desirable residence among the bushes'.

At Lansdowne's Hallowe'en Party, 'everyone dressed in what they imagined fashions would be in the year 2000', whilst £900 raised from the Spring Sale and other fund-raising events was used to purchase new stage-curtains and a film-projector—with sound! A 'flu epidemic in the Spring term caused the boarders to be sent home two weeks early, and Miss Drever Smith described poor health as 'an impediment to progress' within the School. 'Flu, measles, chicken-pox, mumps, and German measles had caused attendance to fall below 50 per cent at times during the session, and 'no sooner had the doors opened' at the new sanatorium, than 'the patients poured in'.

Meanwhile, on the sporting front, whilst hockey and netball were being played in the winter, lacrosse had been discontinued. In the summer, the West of Scotland Schools' Tennis Tournament was instigated, whilst at the Mudhook Races, St Bride's won the Christie Cup for Girls' Schools.

The prizes were presented in 1959 by Miss Isobel Sinclair, only the second woman in Scotland to have become an advocate at that time. She reminded those present that: 'School is a small world, and . . . outside it is a man's world still, rudely and jealously guarded by men.' Women were, she felt, 'still finding (their) feet in this world of equality . . . life for a modern woman is a very complicated business, but . . . never so good and never so exciting.'

Into The Sixties

1960 saw two whole-day holidays to celebrate Prince Andrew's birth and Princess Margaret's wedding. The Princess also visited Helensburgh to open the Services' Canteen, and the whole School assembled at the station to watch her drive away.

More modern technology arrived in the School in the shape of a 'portable transistor wireless-set' and 'Two record-players, one for dancing and one for language-work', whilst a number of films were shown on the new projector. Another mock election was won by the Conservative candidate, with the Liberal in second place: 'There was little support for the Labour candidate and less for the Communist.' At Ashmount's Hallowe'en Party, 'Miss Smith, dressed as a witch, told . . . fortunes and handed out potatoes with trinkets in them from a cauldron. The juniors were a bit scared but thought the potatoes were worth it.'

Lansdowne was rewired and 'Nightstore' heaters were installed, whilst at the Inter-School Swimming Gala, the Junior team won the Coronation Bowl for the seventh year running. The School was saddened by the death of Miss Emlyn, who had taught History for eleven years, and who had 'revitalised' the Day Girls' House.

Presenting the prizes, Lady Lithgow commented that teachers were metaphorically 'packing bags for others setting out on a long journey. The travellers might not know what would be best to pack.'

In 1961, the Burnbrae Dining-Room had to be gutted after the discovery of dry rot; the Ashmount Hallowe'en Party was won by 'The Flowerpot Men', whilst at Woodend's Firework Party, where lessons had obviously not been learnt from Lansdowne's 1955 experience, a spark in the box caused '. . . a wonderful mixed display of shooting rockets, crackers, whizzing cartwheels and brightly-coloured Roman candles, all blazing at once. It was very exciting.' Woodend had also been unlucky with their pets, as Toby the tortoise, who had been given to the girls the previous year by 'the daily maid', found 'the rolling-skating in the conservatory too much for him, when he was hibernating, and one morning (they) found him dead'. A replacement pet, a hamster, also escaped without trace.

There were ongoing discussions about the costs of *The Bridesian* magazine, and the names of those in arrears with their subscriptions (32 in all) were to be printed in the magazine. The list of members' names and addresses had been cut to save space, and this information was to be printed as a separate booklet every three years. However, Miss Drever Smith supported the retention of the creative-writing section, which was also in danger of being cut to save costs.

At Clarendon there were plans to install a new 'teaching kitchen', as Domestic Science was to become an 'O' Grade subject. ('O' Grades were now scheduled to begin in 1962. 1961 was to be the last year of the Scottish Leaving Certificate.) Meanwhile, a 27" TV

Senior girls in the uniform of the 1950s / early 1960s, including gloves and Dexter hats.

set had been purchased by the School so that the girls could 'see some of the events of national importance as they occur'.

By 1962 the new Domestic Science Room in Clarendon had opened. It contained six kitchen 'bays', each with its own washing-machine. Equipment was moved from Lansdowne, where the Department had been located previously. A debate against Hermitage Academy argued the motion that 'It Would Be Better For Britain to Join With America Than With The Common Market', whilst the School also entered the English-Speaking Union Debating Contest for the first time. The Duke of Edinburgh's Award Scheme was opened to girls, and the School's pass-rate at Higher was 87 per cent.

In 1963, new laboratories, (the present Physics Labs, which were refurbished in 2001) were under construction. The development had perhaps been prompted by the new SCE

The new (1963) Physics laboratory.

syllabi for Physics and Chemistry, which also led to the School employing for the first time three specialist science teachers, one each for Chemistry, Physics and Biology. The old laboratory, in Paterson's 1908 extension, became a Geography room (Music in 2002).

The School had its biggest-ever roll in S.5 and S.6, and said goodbye, permanently as it seemed at the time, to Miss M. Rawlins who had taught in the Nursery and was leaving for Germany. The playing-fields were unusable due to bad weather throughout the whole of the Spring term, and there was skating on the blaes hockey pitch. A 'twist' (dance) competition was held to raise money for charity, and Lansdowne girls had 'many hours of enjoyment' from their new transistor radio. A party visited Greenock to witness the launching of a replica of Henry Bell's *Comet*, whilst at the Inter-School Swimming Gala, the Junior team retained the Coronation Bowl for the tenth year in succession. The first Bronze Duke of Edinburgh certificates were also awarded to St Bride's pupils.

In 1964 the School received some publicity when it was featured in the *Scottish Field* magazine, in a feature that included several pages of photographs. Miss Drever Smith was quoted as saying that St Bride's 'allocated quite a bit of time' to dress-making, 'so that the academic side is modified . . .'. She also added that: 'There are times when I wonder whether I'm a factor or a school mistress', a comment with which Mr Ian McKellar, Assistant Head and Master of Works in 2003, would have much sympathy.

By January, the new laboratories had been finished, and they were formally opened by

Sir Angus Cunninghame Graham, Lord Lieutenant of Dunbartonshire, and his wife, on 8 February. The new accommodation comprised a physics laboratory, a chemistry laboratory, a preparation room, and cloakrooms; St Bride's was fortunate to be the first of the Girls' Company Schools (which were now 3 out of 29 independent schools in Scotland to be receiving a Direct Grant from the Government) to have new laboratories. Sir David Anderson, former Director of the Royal Technical College in Glasgow, who had acted as advisor, stated that science '. . . at one time had not been thought to be a necessary subject in a girl's education', but now 'new and exciting careers had opened up for women in many directions'. After Lady Cunninghame Graham had cut the ribbon and declared the laboratories open, experiments were carried out to demonstrate the new equipment, and the party then proceeded to Clarendon for tea.

At Speech Day, Miss Drever Smith referred to an increase in the roll (there were 120 boarders, approximately one-third of the total), particularly in S.5 and S.6, which was due, she felt, to the girls' success at 'O' Grade. She also commented prophetically on the increased educational use of machines: 'radio, T.V., tape-recorder, projector . . . pupils often prove handier and more experienced than the staff.' It was even rumoured that there was a 'machine to do long multiplication'!

The School also underwent its second inspection in Miss Drever Smith's time; in addition, athletics' colours were awarded for the first time, and eight girls received Duke of Edinburgh Silver Awards. A programme of lectures was held on a weekly basis for S.6; one of the topics was racial discrimination. A Shakespearean evening was also held to celebrate the 400 years since the poet's birth; those present read sonnets, sang madrigals and danced quadrilles. Burnbrae leavers presented a set of bathroom scales, which proved to be 'very popular and much used by everybody . . .'.

In the outside world, the Robbins' *Report*, to which Sir David Anderson was a contributor, proposed the creation of half a million university places in total, the increase being due to the fact that there were 'large resources of talent as yet . . . untapped'. Girls in particular were not taking advantage of available opportunities in areas such as science, and 'were yet to exploit their real capabilities in some of the professions'. Dr Curran, presenting the prizes in June, also prophetically referred to education as 'a great industry of the future', and suggested that there was a need for a university in the Highlands.

1965 witnessed another mock election, *The Bridesian* magazine suggesting that St Bride's was 'the safest Tory seat in the country'. The first School Dance was also held; it was for S.5 and S.6 pupils (there were a record 29 girls in S.5), and the hope was expressed (and has subsequently been realised), that the occasion would join Sports Day (cancelled due to bad weather that year) and Speech Day as permanent fixtures in the School calendar.

The death of Sir Winston Churchill (who had once written personally to girls at Lansdowne thanking them for a birthday present which they had sent him) was marked by a Memorial Service, whilst on a lighter note, Woodend had acquired a record player and held 'twisting competitions'. Woodend also held its Christmas Party in January, painting the bare tree white in an effort to create a festive mood. The Fruin Award for Public Speaking was presented for the first time, and Miss Sharp and Miss Stockdale (the latter was also a former pupil) left after more than twenty years' service each.

101

At Speech Day, the Headmistress referred to the changing patterns of women's lives, in particular to the trend of returning to work after children had grown up. Miss E. Rennie, Principal of Craigie College of Education in Ayr, also remarked that:

> The educated woman today is a highly privileged person in a world where education still is a possession of so small a minority . . . . The married woman . . . must learn to live intelligently a double life because her help is so badly needed in the world.

In the background, the Government's plans for comprehensive education were looming, and there were fears that the Direct Grant Schools would be absorbed into the state system. By 1966, plans had been submitted to the Local Authority for the long-awaited new gymnasium, and work was soon to begin. A mock election somewhat surprisingly elected a Liberal, whilst the Debating Team reached the finals of *The Scottish Daily Express* competition; in swimming, the Senior team won the Fruin Shield at the Inter-Schools' Gala. Meanwhile, the town was hit by a virus in January and February, and it was reported that 'the School Sanatorium had never before been so full'. There were 29 girls in S.6, making it the largest in Miss Drever Smith's time, and probably in the School's history; there was a record number of applicants from the School for university, and St Bride's also achieved a record number of 'A' grades at Higher. Additionally, the School also had two male members of staff, apparently the first ever, whilst Mr G.N. Ferguson became Chairman of the Girls' School Company.

The prefects of 1965 outside the east door.
Centre left: Susan Taylor, Head Girl. Centre right: Diana Heron, Vice-Captain.

At Speech Day, Miss Drever Smith commented on the difficulty for the professional educator of 'keeping abreast of change', (even more difficult in 2003), whilst Mrs Whittaker, presenting the prizes, emphasised the importance for girls of following a career before marriage, so that they could return to it later. By September 1967 the new gymnasium was completed, although cloakrooms, showers and changing facilities were not to be added until the following year.

A 'June Jamboree' was also held to raise money for a new Sports' Pavilion, to replace the old one pictured on page 65. The sideshows and stalls in the School grounds raised over £2,000, which was perhaps some compensation for the fact that the Labour Government froze the levels of Direct Grant. Meanwhile, S.5 Physics pupils represented Scotland in the National Finals of the Schools' Project Competition at the London Science Fair, whilst the Debating Team reached the finals of the *Daily Express* Competition. Debates held in School during the year included: 'Pirate Radio Stations Should be Banned'; 'The Americans Should Leave Vietnam'; 'The Space Race is Worth the Effort'; 'Man is Master of the Household'; 'A Housewife Does Not Benefit From A Degree', and 'There Are Too Many Foreign Students At Scottish Universities'; (these topics were perhaps a strange amalgamation of the 'swinging sixties' and the previous era). Other events of note included Woodend's 'Black and White Minstrel Show' (too politically incorrect for today), and the retiral of Miss Atkinson after 38 years of teaching at St Bride's. A decision was also taken to continue with the London Board's G.C.E. 'A' Levels for S.6 pupils, rather than to adopt the S.E.B.'s new Certificate of Sixth Year Studies, the development of which, however, the School would 'watch with interest'. Thirty years later, Lomond was faced with the same choice: to continue with 'A' Levels or to switch to the S.Q.A's Advanced Higher in 1999; the decision taken was the same.

1968 was a year of student unrest, at home and abroad. Miss Drever Smith had no fears for St Bride's leavers, however, who, she stated, had '. . . qualities of heart and head which would keep them safely on course'. It was also fifty years since women first obtained the vote. The new Sports' Pavilion was finished, and the games' field drained, whilst 30 girls took part in a fifty-mile sponsored walk for Christian Aid. Despite the fact that only two of the thirty finished the walk, £500 (at an old penny per mile) was raised for the charity. This year also saw the formation of the Housebound Club, which was to provide entertainment and hospitality for the elderly for the next 25 years, and sadly, the death of Jean Stockdale, former pupil, member of staff, and Guild President. Miss Stockdale had been Head of Science from 1945 to 1964. Her bequest of £200 provided an annual prize for progress in Science (which today is awarded to the most outstanding scientist), and an onyx clock for the Library.

By 1969, rising costs of production meant that the magazine had to be drastically pruned in size. The School section was published minus creative-writing pieces, photographs and illustrations, but the pruning was to no avail, since the 1968–69 edition was to be the last edition of *The Bridesian* in the format in which it had been published since 1911. (The printing bill had been paid only with the help of the Directors, who warned that such circumstances 'must never happen again'.) This year also saw the retirement of Miss Cameron after 18 years as Head of Music, and the formation of a School Council, which allowed elected pupil members to discuss with staff any issues concerning them about the running of the School. Council members were to prove valuable when they took over the organisation of the School Sale when one third of the staff were absent with 'flu. (The School Council concept was again put into practice in 1999.)

The Last Few Years

1970 was the first in 60 years in which a School Magazine had not been published. The Headmistress suggested separating Guild and School contributions into separate magazines in future, whilst the English Department argued (perhaps rather grandiosely) for the retention of a creative writing section, which provided '. . . an outlet for thought and feeling . . . as an alternative to . . . undirected social revolt . . . lighting the candles of (pupils') imagination in our darkening world.'

More importantly, there were also worries about the future of the School, but the election of a Conservative government (which was reflected in the result of the School's own mock election) postponed the Labour Party's plans for large-scale integration of fee-paying and Direct Grant schools into the comprehensive system; the Direct Grant was restored, although at a level lower than that operating in the 1960s, and Miss Drever Smith was able to state that 'the future of St Bride's seems secure'. Things were soon to change, however, as the frequent changes of Government in the 1970s saw dramatic swings of policy towards private education.

Other notable events were the retirement of Miss Janet Barbour after 39 years as Head of the Preparatory Department, the opening of the new showers in the gymnasium changing-rooms, and the fiftieth anniversary of Burnbrae as a School boarding-house, which was celebrated by a party to which all former Burnbrae House-Captains were invited. Former Headmistress Miss Hensman, by now Sister Mary Frideswide, gave a talk to the School about her religious calling, and six S.6 girls cruised to the West Indies in December on the SS *Nevasa*, which sailed from Southampton. (In all, 1,000 children were on this 'educational cruise'.) 1970 was also marked by a half-holiday in recognition of former pupil Margaret Shearer's First Class Degree in Greek and Sanskrit.

In 1971, financial pressures continued to bite. There was a national shortage of teachers, and staff turnover in most schools was high. Miss Drever Smith praised her staff, whose thoughts were '. . . what can I do for the School . . . ?' and who provided a continuity 'very unusual at this time'. In evidence of this dedicated long-service, Miss Tinley, who had been School nurse for 17 years, retired, as did Miss Gillespie, House Mistress of Woodend for over 16 years. Meanwhile, Woodend was sold, the junior boarders housed there moving to Lansdowne, and as a further cost-cutting exercise, the Sanatorium was also closed. The Headmistress moved into Ashmount with S.6, the idea being to help prepare the girls, who had their own study-bedrooms, for student life. The departure of S.6 girls from Lansdowne meant that space was freed for the construction of further bathrooms and showers, and a new dormitory with a carpet, 'a luxury which outsiders envied', was created.

Further costs were incurred by the essential work that had to be carried out to ensure that fire-control standards were met in all buildings, whilst national strikes caused power-cuts that in turn led to the cancellation of the School Dance and House-parties. (These events were eventually held during the summer term.) Junior boarders were also sent home a week early at Christmas.

In addition, the year was also marked by a series of Open Days at Clarendon; the introduction of the national 'Thistle Award' scheme for athletics; St Bride's first appearance at the Dunbartonshire County Sports, and the opening of an 'animal house' for 'School pets', in particular, locusts, stick-insects and mice. An Ashmount boarder wrote, between clenched teeth perhaps: 'It fell to Ashmount to feed them during the weekend. Most of us will, I am sure, remember with feeling the locusts.'

1972 saw the retirement of Miss Drever Smith after 19 years as Headmistress. At the Prize-Giving, held at Old and St Andrew's Church (the West Kirk), Head Girl Irene Stark stated that Miss Drever Smith had been 'good to us, but most of all . . . good for us'. The Directors also praised the departing Headmistress, who had made a 'truly distinguished contribution to the history of the School', and at a dinner in her honour presented her with a gold necklace. The Guild's present was a silver wine salver and a cheque, which Miss Drever Smith used to buy a transistor radio. The pupils gifted a green marble clock. On her part, the departing Headmistress was 'steadily optimistic' about the future of the School. St Bride's was, she said, 'Clyde-built to withstand whatever comes against her.' She also referred at her presentation to her dream of:

> . . . a new building . . . a hall . . . a centre for all kinds of activity . . . a building with great windows so that it was full of light . . . a marvellous evocation of the future . . . space and light . . . freedom with order . . . .

Thus she prophetically summed-up the new School of 1998, in particular, the new Larchfield Hall.

Miss Drever Smith was succeeded by Miss Christine Campbell, Headmistress of Richmond Lodge School in Belfast, who had previously taught at St Columba's, Kilmacolm. It was suggested that the new Headmistress would find it 'a pleasant change to be in a part of the world where one can go out on to the streets without fear of a bomb explosion'.

Guild funds were still in difficulties, however, and subscriptions consequently had to be increased, but in her departing speech, Miss Drever Smith praised the existence of the Guild, stating that, 'women

Miss Christine Campbell, Headmistress of St Bride's, 1972–1976.

take a much less sentimental view of their old schools than men'. The year was also noteworthy for the death of several people who had been prominent for many years in the life of the School: Miss King, who had been Housemistress at Burnbrae and Head of English for 28 years, (she had retired in 1947); Mr Walter Blackie, Director for over 25 years, and Chairman of the local Directors; and Mr W. Maxwell Simmers, a Director for 20 years. Meanwhile, to help the School's finances, as the Direct Grant had been cut once again, the plot of land north of the burn at Burnbrae was sold, whilst Mrs H. Mack became Chair of the Girls' School Company.

1973 saw the retirement of William Sorley after fifty years of service as a gardener at Woodend and Lansdowne, (Mr Sorley had been one of five gardeners at Lansdowne when

Miss Orr in the classroom that later became the School's first Computing laboratory.
25 pupils are visible, and it seems likely that there is at least one more row of girls at the back.

it was still a private house), and of Miss Nesbitt, Housemistress at Burnbrae and Head of Maths for 28 years. The roll stood at over 400, and two new classrooms (the present Nursery) were built in the grounds of Clarendon for the P.6 classes. 'House' competitions were organised, the new houses being Endrick, Fruin and Leven, and a record was produced by the three School choirs, being '. . . greeted with considerable acclaim'. (The choirs sang 'Sing We Merrily, Sing We Sadly' under the direction of music teacher Kenneth Macintosh. The record sold for £2.40.)

In 1974 there was a 25 per cent fee-increase due to the freezing of Government grants, and the Directors warned that termly reviews of fees might be required. There was also dwindling interest in the affairs of the Guild, and finances still threatened the production of the *Guild Magazine*, which had continued to be published as a much-reduced separate entity after the cessation of the School magazine. Guild President Lillian Gray felt, however, that there was still '. . . a nucleus of members to whom the Guild is meaningful', and who supported its joint aims of helping charities and linking Bridesians.

Reorganisation led to the old gymnasium (the present Music Studio) becoming an Art room, (complete with gallery), whilst the Art Studio (now Mrs Brown's T.2 classroom), became a classroom and careers' library. Meanwhile a new physics laboratory was formed from one of the east wing classrooms previously used for Primary 7, whilst the other P.7 room in the east wing became an English classroom (Dr Everett's in 2003).

The year was also marked by the retirement of Miss Frances Orr, who had taught French and German at the School for 38 years, and who had been Second Mistress for 24 years. The School was losing, through retirement, many of the staff who had, as Miss Drever Smith had said in 1971, provided continuity and who linked the School to its past.

A national teacher shortage and runaway inflation led to strike action in the state sector in 1974, and to a 30 per cent pay increase for teachers (the 'Houghton Award') in 1975. The salary-increase was backdated, and was coupled with a reduction of Government Grants, which were to disappear entirely in 1982. (In the event, the Conservative Government elected in 1979 phased the grant out by 1986, and replaced it with the Assisted Places Scheme.) The effect on St Bride's, and other small private schools, was disastrous. In January 1975, St Bride's fees were increased by 56 per cent, with a resultant loss of pupils, although 'not as many' as Miss Campbell 'had feared'. (The roll still stood at around 400.) Fewer girls stayed on into S.6, and fewer entered Clarendon. Larchfield, of course, was suffering from similar problems, which were exacerbated by its much smaller roll. A merger was mooted, and a working-party was set up. By the time of Prize-Giving in June, Miss Campbell was able to state categorically that the merger was going ahead:

What the next few years will bring, no one can tell. We are going ahead with our plans to amalgamate with Larchfield, but they will naturally take time to work out.

She added that the year had been a 'very difficult' one for St Bride's, and that without the merger, 'the problems were unlikely to diminish'. The only alternative was to integrate with the state system; however, the Director of Education for Strathclyde informed the Directors of the Girls' School Company that, after consideration of the Company's three schools, it had been decided that only some of St Bride's buildings met Strathclyde's criteria, whilst none of Park or St Columba's facilities did so. As a result, all three schools reverted to independent status.

Larchfield

The origin of Larchfield Academy (as it was known until 1900, when it became Larchfield School) predated that of Helensburgh High School by 50 years. The present building was completed in 1858, one year before Ardenlee, but the School existed in various forms before this date, operating in the 1840s in Burnside House on the corner of Campbell Street and Argyle Street (which was previously a school run by the Rev. Arthur), and in Colquhoun Villa in Colquhoun Street. The year of foundation is given as 1845 in the final edition of the School magazine, *The Larchfield Review*, and also in an article that appeared in *The Helensburgh and Gareloch Times* in July 1910, entitled: 'Larchfield School: A Brief History'. It was owned by the blind Rev. D.G. Wardlaw until 1855, (although apparently Dr Graham became Headmaster in 1848). Dr Graham was succeeded by Rev. Wardlaw's son-in-law, James S. Scott, who also purchased the newly-built Larchfield Academy from Rev. Wardlaw in 1858. The initial roll included girls. By 1861, the School had 29 boarders. In 1864, Mr Scott was succeeded by Mr Alex MacKenzie, who by the following year had expanded the number of day-pupils to more than 70. He also extended the building. By 1876, there were 37 boarders and 100 day-boys, and this appears to have been Larchfield's high-point in terms of roll. Upper Ardencaple, now the site of Lomond's rugby pitches, was acquired by Larchfield during the period of Mr MacKenzie's headship, whilst the West Room and the porch were added to the building. The first Academical Dinner was held in the Queen's Hotel in 1877.

In 1881, Mr Thomas Bayne, the school's English and Classics master, succeeded Mr Mackenzie. He was responsible for the erection of the new gymnasium (Lomond's former dining-hall) at the rear of the School, but also focused on examination success more than had previously been the case. Mr Bayne was a strict disciplinarian who is alleged to have spied on both staff and pupils, although the tall hat that he habitually wore usually gave him away when in hiding!

In 1900, Mr Bayne was succeeded by Mr John R.H. Newitt, and the School became a Limited Company. The School's aims, according to *The Helensburgh and Gareloch Times* were to prepare boys for '. . . commercial life or for entering universities, Army, Navy or Civil Service, and to cultivate (their) moral and physical development . . .', whilst school life under Mr Newitt became, according to the newspaper, 'a joy'. However, the roll was falling, and on Mr Newitt's departure in 1910 to establish a preparatory school for boys in 42 acres at Shandon House, *The Helensburgh and Gareloch Times* commented that both Larchfield and St Brides, which were '. . . recognised as an absolute necessity to the well-being and prosperity of . . . Helensburgh' required 'a more active interest on the part of the general community'. The writer of the article believed that expansion in boarding numbers was essential for both schools; (this would be brought about by social circumstances during World War One), and bemoaned the fact that: '. . . few there are who take an active interest in promoting (the two School's) prosperity.' However, the School prospered during the 1920s, when a science laboratory was constructed along with 2 further internal storeys.

Mr Newitt's successor was Mr Charles Dunlop, who had been educated at Merchiston Castle School and Oxford University. Other twentieth century Headmasters included Messrs. Monfries; Perkins; Pagden; Clark; (Rev.) S.T. Hutchinson; Widdowson, and Howard.

A number of famous personalities have been connected with the School over the years, most notably, of course, John Logie Baird, the inventor of television, and his friend, the actor Jack Buchanan, who were both pupils. (They also attended St Bride's kindergarten.) Sir James Frazer was also a pupil, whilst poets C. Day-Lewis and W.H. Auden taught at the School briefly in the late 1920s and early 1930s. In 1967, Auden responded to a Larchfield Appeal by sending a cheque for 50 dollars to Headmaster John Widdowson from his home in Austria. He added in a footnote to his letter, 'I trust that your staff are better fed than they were in my day.'

Back at St Bride's, financial worries finally saw the end of the *Guild Magazine*, the final edition being typed rather than properly printed; even money for posting copies to members was a problem. On a brighter note, however, the 80th anniversary of the School was celebrated by a tea-party, whilst the Lomond Association (today the P.T.A.) was formed, and all S.6 pupils received unconditional offers of university places. The hockey team toured Holland with Miss Husband, (later to be Mrs Clark), and Miss J. Howie (who retired in 2001); the School also won the Dunbartonshire Schools' Public Speaking Competition.

The year was notable too for the death of Miss Bell, former Headmistress, 33 years after her retiral. Miss Bell had taken the School into its second phase, and had always had a vision of an enlarged St Bride's, a vision which would come to pass after the fire, in 1998, 23 years after her death. Tributes to the former Headmistress praised her as a 'teacher rather than an administrator', with a strong sense of occasion.

Larchfield Academy boarders, c.1860.

John Graeme Anderson, pupil at Larchfield c.1900.
John was the elder son of William Anderson, who was a Director of both St Bride's and Larchfield Schools. John Anderson later became Chairman of the Governors of Larchfield.

Larchfield Academy.

HEAD-MASTER:

THOMAS BAYNE, (St Andrews), F.S.A., Scot.

Advanced Classics and English........	Mr Bayne.
Classics	Mr E. Barker Prescott, B.A., Cantab. Mr A. W. Reid (Glas. Univ.) Mr W. Edney Peters, A.C.P.
Mathematics ...., Physics .... Chemistry	Mr W. H. Winter, B.A., Cantab. Mr Peters.
English	Mr Barker Prescott, B.A. Mr Winter. Mr Reid. Miss Nellie R. Bayne. Assistants.
Writing and Book-keeping............	Mr Winter and Assistant.
Modern Languages......................	Herr Hübner.
Elocution	Mr W. S. Vallance.
Drawing and Painting....................	Mr James Phillips.
Vocal and Instrumental Music......	Mr W. J. Clapperton. Miss Bayne.
Violin, 'Cello, &c.........................	Mr Thomas Walker.
Fencing and Gymnastics.............. Drill	Professional Master.
Dancing and Deportment......	Professional Master.
Phonography (Script)	Mr Brown.

MASTERS RESIDENT AT LARCHFIELD.

Mr Winter.

Mr Peters.

Session Begins on **THURSDAY,** *September 7th.*

LARCHFIELD SCHOOL

Was Re-constructed and Re-organised in September, 1900, under the Management of

LARCHFIELD LIMITED.

BOARD OF DIRECTORS.

Wm. Anderson, J.P., Inistore, Helensburgh, *Chairman.*
Col. R. Easton Aitken, Lansdowne Park, Helensburgh.
Andrew Bonar Law, M.P., Kintillo, Helensburgh.
A. M. M. G. Kidston, J.P., Clydesdale Bank House, Helensburgh.
Wm. Russell, J.P., Luss Estates Office, Helensburgh.
J. Whitelaw Hamilton, R.S.W., The Grange, Helensburgh.
W. P. Ure, Balvaird, Helensburgh.

THE whole of the Buildings were renovated and put into a most perfect sanitary condition, a New Changing Room and Lavatory being added. A Sanatorium was constructed in June, 1903.

The School Work comprises Modern Languages, Classics, English, and Mathematics, each Section being in charge of a fully qualified Master. The Physical Culture of the Boys is attended to by the Masters, who supervise and arrange Games daily between 2 and 4, either in the Park or the Gymnasium. There is accommodation at present for about 20 Boarders.

THE STAFF OF MASTERS IS—

Headmaster	—John R. H. Newitt, B.A. (Cantab.).
Mathematics	—John R. H. Newitt, B.A. (Cantab.).
Classics	—J. Boyd Robertson, B.A. (Oxon.).
English	—J. W. Forbes, B.A. (Oxon.).
Junior School	—A. W. Reid.
Modern Languages	—P. Hübner.
Music	—T. W. Stanton.
Drawing	—James Phillips.
Shorthand	—William Brown.
Gymnastics	—S. Stewart.
Drill	—Sergt. Henderson.

For Prospectus and particulars apply to
JOHN R. H. NEWITT, B.A., Headmaster,
or to Secretary of the Company, GEORGE R. MURRAY, Municipal Buildings, Helensburgh.

An 1892 advertisement for Larchfield Academy from the *Helensburgh and Gareloch Times*.

An early 1900s advertisement from the *Helensburgh and Gareloch Times* for the renamed Larchfield School, showing Mr William Anderson as Chairman of the Board of Directors.

Larchfield School c.1906. Note that the west section of the building was still single-storey; it was increased in height during the 1920s.

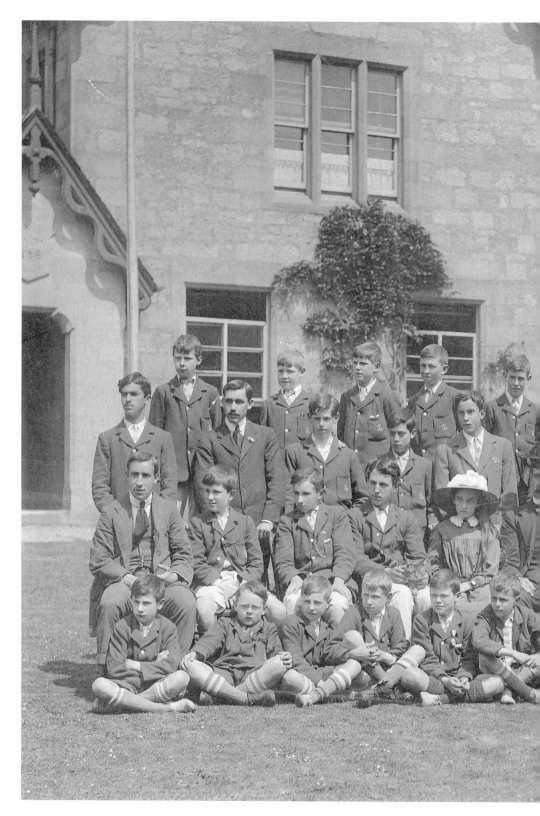

Larchfield School, 1911.
The roll seems to be in the mid-thirties, including several 'Anglo–Indians'.

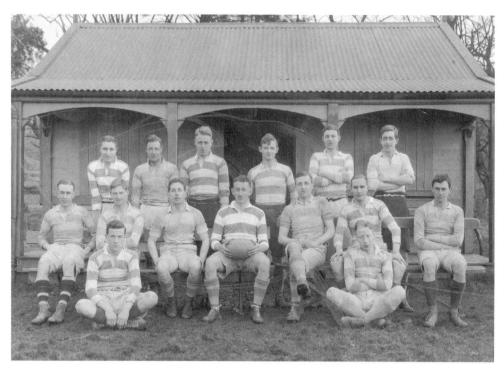

Old Larchfieldians rugby team, 1924–25, showing the pavilion that once stood at the present Lomond rugby pitches.

The extended building, post 1920s.

The recreation room at Larchfield.

The Larchfield gymnasium (Lomond's dining-hall at the time of the 1997 fire).

Larchfield School staff and pupils, c.1930.
The roll is around 40. Fourth from right in the second row from the front is poet W.H. Auden.
(Is C. Day-Lewis fourth from the left in the same row?)

Larchfield School's boarders, 22 March 1936.
Left to right: W. Dobson, J. Worlledge, N. Weir, I. Bowers, J. Robinson, R. Tennant.

A Larchfield classroom, showing the memorial to former pupils who fell in World War One. This plaque now hangs in Lomond's dining and assembly hall—Larchfield Hall.

118

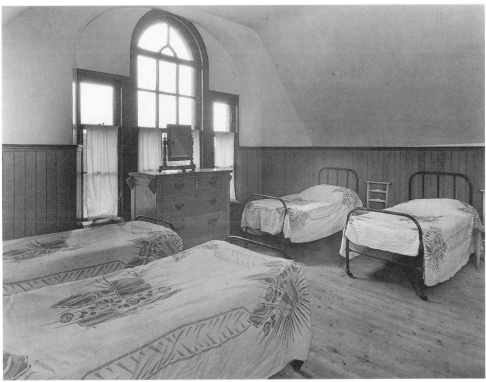

The interior of a dormitory at Larchfield.

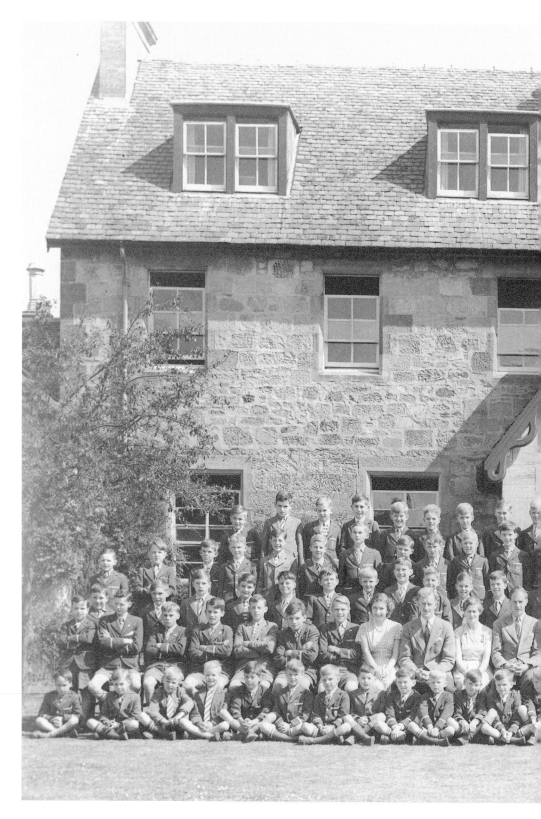

The pupils and staff of Larchfield School in 1955.
A young David Arthur, who twenty-two years later would become the first
Principal of Lomond School, is ninth from the left, second row from the front.

A Larchfield feast.

Larchfield boys at Assembly, clearly showing the school badge.

The new classrooms in the rear playground at Larchfield. These rooms were used for Modern Languages and Technical Drawing during the 1990s.

Taybank in 2000. Formerly the home of Larchfield Headmasters, Taybank became a Senior Boys' Boarding House after the 1977 merger. It was sold in 1981.
(Photo: Mrs E. Maclean.)

Part Four:

Lomond: *Prospiciamus*

In 1976 Miss Campbell was appointed as Headmistress of Albyn School, Aberdeen, and Larchfield Headmaster John Widdowson moved to Keil. Miss Orr returned as Acting Headmistress while Miss Nesbitt also came out of retirement to help the School in its last year. Four boys joined the senior school, and a short-leet for the post of Headteacher of the combined schools was drawn up. There was also a competition to choose the name of the new School (one suggestion being 'Guys 'n' Dolls'!). Burnbrae was full to capacity, with girls as young as P.6 boarding there. In January 1977, the new Headmaster, (or Principal) Mr David Arthur, took up his post to oversee the last two terms of St Bride's existence as a separate entity. Mr Arthur, a graduate of Edinburgh University, had previously taught at Larchfield, and at the time of his appointment was Rector of Greenfaulds Academy in Cumbernauld, one of the largest comprehensive schools in Scotland. In the meantime, the name which had been decided upon for the new School helped both to clarify its geographical whereabouts and to link it with the magnificent surrounding landscape in the minds of the parents of prospective boarders.

Mr David Arthur,
Principal, Lomond School, 1977–1986.

At the final St Bride's Prize Giving, Mr Arthur referred to the day as one of '. . . pride in what has gone before, and of pleasure in anticipation . . .' and spoke of the merger as a 'wedding of true minds'. The Chairman of St Bride's Governors, Mr Peter Paisley, who had attended the School's Kindergarten, stated that Lomond had been formed from '. . . two schools whose spirit had stood the test of time.' St Bride's was '. . . going out on the crest of a wave, with more pupils at the end of the year than at the beginning.'

Another speaker was Sir David Renton, Privy Councillor, Q.C., and M.P. for Huntingdon since 1945, who was Miss Renton's nephew. (Sir David had also attended St Bride's kindergarten.) In honour of the occasion, he granted an extra half-day's holiday the following session.

Although the new school was short of capital, a number of structural alterations were necessary before Lomond could open on 6 September. (Staff were back four days earlier to help clean up.) Larchfield's hall became the dining-hall, and new kitchens had to be

The final St Bride's Prizegiving, June 1977.
The new Lomond Principal, Mr David Arthur, is on the right. Mr Peter Paisley, Chairman of the St Bride's Governors, is third from the left, whilst second from the left is Sir David Renton, MP, nephew of St Bride's first Headmistress, Miss J.B.M. Renton. Third from the right is Mrs Mack, Chair of the Girls' School Company.

Lomond School Staff in the opening (1977–78) session.
Only three of the people in the photograph remain at the School in 2002:
Depute Head Mr W. MacKenzie is eighth from the left in the front row; Head of Music Mrs A. Lyon is
seventh from the right in the middle row, whilst Mrs C. Malan, Transitus teacher, is fifth from the
left, back row. Three other members of staff who completed 25 years' service are: Mrs C. Clark,
seventh from right, front row; Miss J. Howie, third from right, front row; and Mrs E. Drummond,
sixth from right, back row.

created, whilst new toilets and cloakrooms were erected at the rear of Clarendon. In St
Bride's itself, boys' toilets had to be built, whilst the Principal took over the former office
accommodation (on the left of the hall on entering the front door), and the office moved to
the former Headmistress's room on the right of the entrance hall. The Domestic Science
room was relocated in what is now the Science Department (Mr Jennison's Biology Lab.
In 2003). Clarendon lost its P.6 and St Bride's its P.7 pupils to Larchfield, (they were known
as M.1 and M.2), whilst S.1 (M.3) pupils were also based there, in what was seen as the
'Middle School'. Meanwhile, S.2–S.6 were housed in St Bride's, the plan for the first few
years being for each building 'to function as a unit on its own with its own Head of School',
an idea which was perhaps intended to convince Old Larchfieldians and Old Bridesians
that their Schools had not totally disappeared in the reorganisation. Senior posts in the
new school were filled by Michael Howard as Head of Larchfield (which thus combined
the equivalent of P.6–S.1), while Elizabeth Leitch became Head of the Junior School at
Clarendon. As Deputy Principal and Housemaster for the senior girls at Ashmount, Mr
Chris Higgs, from Brentwood School in Essex, was appointed, with Mrs Shepherd holding
the positions of Head of Maths and Senior Mistress. The Management Committee which
was established was completed by the appointment of Lt. Cdr. Roger Ball, from the Navy,
as Bursar and later Clerk to the Governors.

Additionally, the Nursery opened in the old St Bride's Sanatorium, Queen's Cottage (named for the Queen's Silver Jubilee), with 13 pupils; (the cottage also housed the Bursar and the School Doctor). Larchfield itself, (junior boys), in Colquhoun Street, and Taybank, previously the Larchfield Headmaster's house, (senior boys) were added to the boarding-houses. In all, Lomond now possessed ten properties. Technical Drawing was introduced, and a new uniform of blue and grey was adopted, with a blazer badge depicting both the larch tree and St Bride.

The formal opening of Lomond School was marked on 6 September by a service in Old and St Andrew's Church; the roll stood at a healthy 530, despite the fees for the new School exceeding those of both Larchfield and St Bride's. (Books and materials were however included in the fees, which they had not previously been in either School.) Mr Arthur stated that both Schools had gone out 'with their heads high', but added that the rampant inflation of the 1970s had threatened both with eventual closure. There had also been a definite need to provide private education for senior boys in the town; (Larchfield had met this need itself until *c*.1927). Lomond was the product of two well-established Schools, but obviously had to create its own image and reputation. Its existence, Mr Arthur said, was 'the culmination of much planning, organisation and vision for the future', the plans being 'architectural, curricular and theoretical'. He stressed the advantages of coeducation, and of providing locally a School with high standards and a clearly-defined philosophy of education. Lomond would be 'responsive to parental needs', and would function as a partnership between pupils, parents and teachers. An extended school day (till 5.00 p.m.) to provide sports and other activities would give the advantages of boarding education to those still living at home, whilst another innovative idea was the introduction of a staff-development course which looked at various topics and ideas that could expand areas of teaching expertise. This course hosted a number of outside speakers, and it is interesting to note that it also attracted a number of Hermitage Academy staff. Although, according to the Principal, Lomond's birth 'had not been an easy one', the virtues valued by the Victorian founders were 'still to be found in Lomond School'.

Meanwhile, the Larchfield Club and the Bridesian Guild for the former pupils of the Schools had been subsumed into the new Lomond Society, (the Guild donating £1400 to equip the new science laboratory, whilst a further sum of £1000 went to the Society from the balances of the Club and Guild); the Lomond Association, (P.T.A.), had also been established with the aim of improving School facilities, and, specifically, to provide a mini-bus. Plans were also being drawn up for a sixth-year college, to be known as 'Lomond College', the first of its kind in Scotland; these never came to fruition, however.

There was also much discussion on the possible curriculum for the 6th year; one option being mooted was the International Baccalaureate, which combined breadth and depth of study. This vision failed on the practical grounds that no university was prepared to accept it.

1978 saw the first-ever Lomond Staff v Pupils hockey match, (this fixture is still an annual event), with the Staff team boasting a remarkable four ex-internationalists. There was also a Staff v Pupils netball match, whilst Maths teacher Maureen McClure was selected for the British canoeing squad for the 1980 Moscow Olympics. (Miss McClure later married Lomond P.E. teacher Nigel Pennie, now Head of P.E. at Morrison's Academy, Crieff.) For the second time in three years, the School won an athletics Thistle Award for secondary schools with a roll of under 500; many similar awards were to follow in the years to come.

In 1979 there were 107 boarders spread across five houses, (Larchfield, Taybank, Ashmount, Burnbrae and Lansdowne). The number of houses was reduced to four when the top floor of Larchfield was taken out of service as it was regarded as being unsuitable for the purpose in a modern age. The Governors were also aware of the existing disparity between boarding facilities for boys and girls, ('. . . comparative luxury of the girls and the bare necessities of the boys'), and as in 2001, considered purchasing, or even building, another house. However, the costs were prohibitive. Junior girls were moved from Burnbrae to Lansdowne, where another dormitory was created, with senior girls remaining at Ashmount. Senior boys were housed at Taybank, opposite Larchfield, whilst Burnbrae became home to Junior and Middle-School boys. The changes provided places for a maximum of 110 boarders, the Governors being determined to prevent the disappearance of boys' boarding altogether, and to equalise, as far as possible, the numbers of boys and girls in the School.

Mr Arthur also recognised the need for courses of a 'more practical nature' for less academic pupils, (Secretarial Studies would shortly join Technical Drawing on the curriculum), and for social and study areas for S.5 and S.6 pupils to encourage them to stay on at School. Games facilities were also 'limited', according to the Principal, but on the positive side, Mr Arthur felt that Lomond was '. . . dynamic . . . ready to listen to the views of parents and youngsters, and to consider the changing demands of the outside world'. Rather prophetically, in view of the events of 1997, he also commented that Lomond was '. . . a robust school. . . . It takes its knocks and comes up smiling.'

The year was also notable for the launch of the *Lomond Association Newsletter* for parents, which two years later would become *The Newspaper of the Lomond Association*, running for over forty issues until 1998. The first *Newsletter* stated that its purpose was to be 'a forum for opinion,' and to '. . . provide information which will be helpful to parents on a variety of topics'.

Elsewhere in the School, a navigation course was held over ten evenings, and Tam Dalyell and Jim Sillars of the Scottish Labour Party debated Devolution in St Bride's Hall in front of a large audience.

In 1980, the Art Department, which since 1974 had been housed in the Studio, (the original gymnasium), was relocated to Larchfield. The old Art Studio next to the Bridesian Library also had become a classroom six years previously, and an Appeal was now launched to equip it as a Library for the whole School. Meanwhile, the Debating Society discussed a British boycott of the Moscow Olympics on political grounds, and the first School v Society cricket and hockey matches were held; (there had been a tennis match the previous year). Snow and rain meant that half of the School's rugby and hockey matches were lost to the weather, whilst Mr Arthur also commented on the difficulty of Lomond competing in sports against much bigger schools. One of the three internal 'houses', (Buchanan), used to provide a basis for competition in a variety of sports and activities between Lomond's own pupils, was renamed 'Bergius' (with a hard 'g') in honour of Mr Adam Bergius, Chairman of Teachers' Whisky and the first Chairman of Lomond's Board of Governors, who had handed over to his successor, Mr R. Pender. Mr Bergius, who was described as 'a true founder of Lomond School,' commented that:

. . . for the first time since its inception, the School is now on a sound financial basis, and it is not necessary to carry . . . large borrowings.

The year was also notable for the deaths of several people connected with the School in various ways. Colin MacGeorge, who had taught at Larchfield since 1962, died aged 64, and was remembered fondly for his motto 'gentlemen don't and others mustn't'. One of Lomond's first male pupils, John Harper, was tragically killed in a car-crash, and two distinguished former pupils of St Bride's, Dr E.M. Oastler, who had left in 1910 and had worked in the Glasgow Medical Mission in the Gorbals from 1928 until her retirement, and Nance Anderson, M.B.E., who established the School's Lennox and Fruin Prizes and whose family gifted Drumgarve to the town to form the Templeton Library, also passed away.

By 1981, membership of the Lomond Society stood at 403, and golf was added to the list of sports at which the School and Society would compete. A shield, still played for today, was presented by Mrs Lillian Gray for competition between the School and Society at cricket (the school team beat the FPs by 40 runs; the fixture would not take place again until 1986); in addition, a Society Dinner, attended by 70 members, including Mr Arthur and Miss Drever Smith, was held in the School; it was hoped that a similar event could be held every three years. Ties and cravats with the Society motif, designed by pupil Angela Fulton, were also produced.

Mr David Arthur (left) with Miss Rachel Drever Smith and the Revd Steven Hutchinson, former Headmaster of Larchfield, at the 1981 Society Dinner held in St Bride's Hall.

Meanwhile, the Association raised funds for a minibus, a Gala Day in June contributing £2,700 to the cause, and the St Bride's tradition of helping charitable causes was continued when the Association's coffee-morning raised £300 for the war-blinded.

Within a year, the Appeal had raised the sum of £115,000, most of it covenanted, and the new library was set up; additional funds for the School were raised by selling Taybank, which had belonged to Larchfield, part of the grounds of Lansdowne Park for private housing, and Queen's Cottage, in the grounds of Burnbrae. The nursery was moved to Clarendon, and the School Doctor to the top of Larchfield. The Bursar was relocated to St Bride's.

New clubs were proliferating in the School, with a Bagpipe Society, Mountaineering Club, Dance Club and Survival Club (membership of which involved spending a week on an island in Loch Linnhe with fishhooks, polythene sheeting and a pound of oatmeal for each person), appearing for the first time. A 'Flabby Daddies' Club' was also set up by P.E. teacher Mr Hayton-Williams, an ex-Marine Commando.

In addition, The Duke of Edinburgh Award Scheme was introduced for all S.3 pupils, the Lomond Association organised a talk for parents on the subject 'Drugs, School and the Home', whilst the Association's *Newsletter* became a *Newspaper*, self-financing through the advertisements that it carried. Rather more controversially, the Association successfully negotiated the instigation of 'Class Meetings', in which a solitary teacher met with all the parents of a given class to discuss the curriculum and other issues of interest to parents. Nationally, there were moves to finally abolish corporal punishment in Scottish schools (although it was not in any case used at Lomond). Dry-rot in Lansdowne led to girls having to queue for baths and showers in Larchfield, whilst the year was also marked by the deaths of former Headmistress Miss Campbell; of Sir David Anderson, Director of the Girls' School Company from 1959–1970, and of Mrs Hilda Purvis, who as Hilda Hamilton

Demolition prior to the construction of the new PE changing rooms, 1982.

had been one of the first pupils when the School moved to St Bride's; (the daughter of one of 'The Glasgow Boys' school of artists, Mrs Purvis had become Chairman of the Guild, and her family donated the Purvis Cup for Art, which is still presented annually, in her memory).

By 1982, the roll stood at 520, with Lomond's then largest-ever Sixth Form of 40. Mr R. Pender, Chairman of the Governors since 1980, remarked that: 'We have set out to market the School.' (This was clearly a novel idea.) He added that: 'Any member of staff who is less than helpful or less than enthusiastic about extra-curricular activities is lower on our scale of approval'.

Dry-rot was discovered in Lansdowne and St Bride's, and a cold spell at the end of the Christmas holidays produced burst pipes in all of the School's properties, those in Ashmount necessitating the evacuation of the nine senior girl boarders. (The small fire that occurred in Clarendon later in the year perhaps served to dry the building out!)

A number of developments were also underway on the buildings' front; two Physics laboratories were equipped, partly from the Appeal proceeds, and partly thanks to the efforts of the Science staff. One of these laboratories was the former Home Economics room. The former Physics laboratory became a Biology room, whilst the Larchfield Science laboratory was transformed into a new Home Economics room. The P.E. changing rooms were also reconstructed, whilst the new Library next to the Bridesian was equipped and a Sixth Year Centre was established at St Bride's in the rooms previously occupied by the Janitor, Mr MacLeod, which had been the site of the fire of 1937. Fire-precaution work was also carried out at Larchfield and St Bride's.

Elsewhere, the new *Lomond Association Newspaper* received favourable mention in *The Times Educational Supplement*, which remarked that 'Lomond has taken a lead in parent-teacher communications . . . .' The first few issues of the Paper, however, adopted a rather confrontational stance on a number of topics, including the number of teaching days in the School Year. Edition Number Six carried a table showing the number of days' holiday at Lomond over a number of years, and compared the figures to those for other Glasgow independent schools. The table showed that Lomond had offered 168 ½ days of teaching in Session 1979–80, (giving over 18 weeks' holiday), and 179 days in Session 1982–83. On its formation in 1976, the School had agreed to offer 185 teaching days, but since the day continued until 5.00 p.m. and extra-curricular activities were also offered on a Saturday, these extra hours were included in the overall calculation. Parental pressure about 'value for money' led, however, to a firm agreement that the School would be open to pupils on one hundred and eighty-five days each year, and this still applies today. *The Lomond Association Newspaper* stated:

> If it is the case that Lomond staff receive higher salaries than teachers in the State system, and enjoy a better teacher-pupil ratio, parent commitment, and, presumably, easier-maintained discipline, one might hope that we might get a markedly greater quantity of educational provision in return for the money we pay.

(At this point, Lomond's teaching-staff received a salary 5–6 per cent above the equivalent state-school salary; this differential was gradually eroded over the ensuing years so that in 2002 it stood at £250 per annum; an increase is planned for 2003.)

The writer's choice of the word 'quantity' rather than 'quality' was perhaps revealing, and Mr Arthur suggested that what actually happened during the School day was more important than the number of days themselves; terms that were too long led to pupil and staff tiredness.

Another article in the *Newspaper* agreed that '. . .the return is inadequate . . .' from Lomond's favourable pupil-teacher ratio, whilst the Association Chairman stated categorically and perhaps controversially that it was '. . .the responsibility of the School to educate the pupils in accordance with the wishes of the parents'. There was clearly tension at the time between the Governors' long-term wider strategic concerns, the staff's day-to-day preoccupations, and parents' short-term requirements for their own children. Perhaps not surprisingly in the prevailing climate, 'class meetings' were postponed, as staff had asked for more time to plan the 'professional aspects' involved in such meetings with parents. However, an Educational Forum, chaired by Tim Devlin, Director of The Independent Schools Information Service, was held at the School to discuss education at Lomond; in particular, internal communications, public relations and the 'political threat to our national heritage'. Mr Arthur was also considering the grading system that was then applied throughout the School, which parents found confusing, and the pattern of the School Day, with moves towards earlier Games lessons in the afternoon to maximise light in the winter, as had been discussed in 1921; (a 3.25 p.m. finish would be introduced for this reason in 1996).

By this stage in Lomond's development, Mr Arthur was able to state that in his view, a genuine 'Lomond ethos' had evolved, based on 'solid common sense, a sense of humour, hard work, kindly courtesy, and, above all, enthusiasm'. The summer saw the departure of the first pupils who had spent their entire secondary career at Lomond.

Meanwhile, the School now had 13 pupils on the Conservative Government's Assisted Places Scheme, which had been introduced in 1981 to replace the Direct Grant system and which allowed children from less-affluent homes to enjoy a subsidised private education; the School also acquired its first computer; a War-Gaming Club was formed; a survival expedition to the Mull of Kintyre took place; a Fete in June raised £2,000 for books for the new Library, and the Chief of Strathclyde Police Drug Squad, addressing a meeting of parents and staff in St Bride's Hall, stated that: 'Helensburgh has the worst drugs' problem of any town in the west of Scotland except Dunoon'. He added that '. . . the drugs' problem in Helensburgh is mainly a problem of the middle and upper classes'. Mr Arthur reassured the meeting, however, that drugs were not a problem at Lomond.

On the curricular front, Middle School pupils were provided with a double period of 'activities' each week; boys were expected to cook and sew, whilst girls attempted some 'primitive joinery'. An Industrial Conference was also held in School for S.5 and S.6 pupils in an attempt to provide a bridge between the school curriculum and 'the modern world of industry'.

In 1983, Mr Arthur took an interesting look forward to the year 2011, 35 years after the merger was agreed. He was confident that Lomond would still exist, and many of his ideas for the future were remarkably prophetic, although events rather overtook some of the others . . . :

All the buildings will, of course, receive Government grants for preservation under the listed building scheme, but inside, the classrooms will be light, airy, with individual heating controls and carpets. There will be extended space around the Science block for an electronics and computer laboratory, while the library area will have large retrieval systems with much of the material on miniaturised film . . . . A fully equipped audio-visual area and a special remedial block with individualised machine-learning systems will be built. There will still be books, chalk, blackboards, teachers and even a Principal, because at the end of the day, human beings learn best through . . . other human beings, and not from machines. . . . There will always be a place for schools like Lomond, small schools, places where people are important, where there is still an emphasis on hard work, on the values of honesty, and the need for commitment.

Mr Arthur also pointed out, very accurately, that:

There is an insatiable desire among Chinese . . . for British-style independent schooling because it offers a true basis for the development of character and intellect, ... Never mind 1984, let us look forward to 2011, because Lomond will still be around.

The Principal also paid tribute to Miss Edith Kinnear, who retired after teaching History at St Bride's and Lomond for 28 years, commenting that, 'Schools like Lomond owe an unpayable debt to the loyalty and strength of teachers like Edith Kinnear.'

Meanwhile, Lomond had published its first Prospectus, and had hosted its first Student Teacher (visits by whom are now a regular occurrence). Helensburgh was twinned with the French town of Thouars, greatly facilitating educational exchanges, and there were proposals to change holiday dates to provide a week's holiday in October; again, this is now a fixture in the calendar.

Significantly, a proposed merger with Keil School in Dumbarton was abandoned following successful fund-raising by a 'Save Keil' campaign organised by parents and F.Ps. One proposal had been that the newly-merged School would occupy the disused premises of St Peter's College in Cardross, empty since 1976. (This award-winning building designed by Jack Coia, and opened in 1968, is described in Walker and Arneil's *Illustrated Architectural Guide to the North Clyde Estuary* (1992) as '. . . a tour de force of spatial brilliance inside and out . . . the proxy of Le Corbusier is marvellously validated . . .'.) The grounds of the College included a large part of Cardross Golf Club; it belonged to the Archdiocese of Glasgow and had previously been used as a seminary. Plans to turn the building into a hotel had fallen through the previous year, when the cost of purchase had been estimated at £1 million. A major factor in the rejection of the College as a site for the proposed new School was the transport problem; most of Lomond's pupils lived in Helensburgh itself or around the Peninsula. Keil however had 74 boarders and only 47 day pupils. In addition, Lomond, with a maximum projected roll of 600, had no need for extra space at that time.

On the curricular front, the reports of the Munn and Dunning Committees that had been published in 1977 were implemented, leading to the introduction of the new Standard Grade courses which were soon to be disrupted by industrial action over teachers' pay in the state sector. In an article in the *Lomond Association Newspaper*, a parent and prominent educationalist, Dr A. Macbeth, correctly predicted the introduction of modular Highers, the creation of one Examination Board (which came about in 1997 with the merger of the S.E.B. and SCOTVEC), and the abolition of CSYS (which occurred in 1999 with the advent of the Advanced Higher). In a letter to parents, Mr Arthur confirmed that '. . . the main aims of Lomond School are academic . . .' and that '. . . the commitment to the Scottish system of examination shall remain'. Academic Commendations and Academic Ties were introduced, and are still awarded today, whilst a second Educational Forum was held, over fifty questions being received in advance. On the subject of corporal punishment, (a topical issue at the time; it was abolished in Scottish schools in 1986), Mr Arthur commented: 'I believe corporal punishment to be inappropriate in a co-educational school and within the context of our powerful parental support.' He added that:

> We live in an age that encourages rebellious attitudes . . . is essentially irreligious . . . allows widespread drug-taking, (including alcohol) . . . does not disapprove of casual relationships, dress or behaviour, and does not like physical punishment. . . . Lomond has always looked for, and has received, a high standard of behaviour from its pupils.

Mr Arthur went on to stress the importance of common goals, shared between the School and parents, and referred to the 'powerful force exerted by the pupils themselves' on behaviour. He concluded that '. . . the price of discipline is eternal vigilance'.

He also emphasised the School's vulnerability to recession:

> Helensburgh is a dormitory town with a large proportion of executives who are forced to move when businesses close . . . a major cause of the drop in the School's roll over the last year.

As an illustration of population mobility, the Principal pointed out that between the years 1978 and 1984, 21 of the then current S.4 year-group had left the School, whilst another 23 new pupils had entered that stage; the S.3 year-group had lost 17 pupils in the same period (out of 33 in 1978), but had gained another 41 children.

Elsewhere in the School, Burnbrae became the proud owner of a computer; a War-Gaming Society, a 'Dungeons and Dragons' Society and a fencing club were formed, whilst an Ashmount boarder commented in the School magazine that '. . . we are thinking of opening the Ashmount kitchen to the public, to educate people in remote Scottish history'. Sadly, 1983 also saw the death of Miss Joan Robertson, who had taught English and Geography at St Bride's from 1926–1960.

In 1984, Mr Arthur stressed the need for efficient marketing, if the School was to prosper. He had travelled 10,000 miles and held eleven marketing sessions in seven months, mainly in the form of local forums, but also including a trip to Kenya, when six schools were visited. The Principal commented that:

> Products do not sell without . . . good marketing . . . Lomond is becoming fairly professional. Marketing is made possible because the School has something of real value to offer . . . . Very good academic results . . . hockey and rugby teams . . . dance, choral and dramatic productions.

A further aid to the School's marketing strategy was the new Computing Laboratory, housed in the old Room 11, formerly Room 16, see p. 106, which had been rewired, refloored and re-equipped with twelve BBC micro-computers, thanks to an Appeal which had raised £15,000, much of it covenanted. The total included a donation of £2,000 from the Association. In addition, Larchfield also possessed a BBC computer, purchased from the proceeds of a Middle School Sponsored Spell which raised £1,300 (a video-recorder and video-camera were purchased from this sum too). Clarendon also had a Spectrum. Interestingly, the Dumbarton Division Advisor for Computing, addressing the Association, pointed out that in 1980 it was estimated that there had only been 20 computers in schools throughout the whole of Scotland. He also predicted the advantages of networking, which arrived at Lomond in the new building of 1998, and also, accurately suggested that examinations in computing were on the horizon. Mr Arthur stressed, however, that '. . . computing skill is no substitute for the old-fashioned mainliners of English, Maths, French and the Sciences . . .' but this did not prevent an evening class being offered for parents who wished to become computer-literate.

At another Educational Forum, Mr MacKenzie spoke in favour of more pupils from Europe, an idea that would come to fruition in the 1990s with a steady influx of pupils from Germany, whilst Mr Murray, Vice-Principal, advocated business-sponsorship for individual children. Extra lessons after school for weak examination-candidates were also discussed, and Mr Arthur stated: 'The School's view is that parents can always ask for extra help, and when it is agreed that such help is necessary, then additional fees would not be charged.' (Again, this was an idea that was to bear fruit in 1996, with the introduction of extra lessons for borderline Higher classes.) Rather oddly perhaps, the reintroduction of cricket, a sport which had petered out after the merger, (it had been a major sport at Larchfield), was also raised at the Forum. The reply was that there were no plans to revive the game, although this statement proved premature.

Meanwhile, girl boarders vacated Ashmount after 68 years, and boys moved in. Burnbrae had its own disco, ('Omega'), and boarding-house competitions were held in hockey, table-tennis, darts, rifle-shooting and general knowledge. (All of these competitions were won by the boys.)

An interesting scientific innovation at this time was the 'Great Easter Egg Race', an event which was held periodically for the next ten years. The aim was for teams of pupils to devise a method of propelling a 'size 5 hen's egg' a distance of five metres, unbroken,

Robb Scott, right, Lomond's first schoolboy rugby internationalist, representing Scottish Schools in 1984. His shirt was framed and still hangs in the School.

using a rubber band as the means of propulsion. Marks were awarded for 'ingenuity, originality, elegance of design, speed, and "giggle-factor"'. The winning design used cardboard wheels and a Meccano frame, and was awarded first prize by Dr Leaf, a retired Lecturer in Physics. Meanwhile, a non-uniform (or 'civvies') day raised £311 for Oxfam's Ethiopian Appeal; the graffiti of many generations were removed from classroom desks, and the new Lomond Association Chairman called for Parent-Governors to be appointed by the Association.

By 1985 the roll had fallen somewhat to around 490 (although it was still 50 more than the 1980 figure), only 50 of whom had attended either St Bride's or Larchfield. (Children who were in P.5 at the time of the merger were now in S.6.); Mr R. Kinloch, the Chairman of the Governors, stated that he would like to recruit a further 50–100 day pupils. Interestingly, whilst the roll of the Senior School, housed in St Bride's, had increased from 213 in 1977 to 266, the roll of the Middle School in Larchfield had fallen from 169 to 123, and that of Clarendon from 150 in 1977 to 98. Mr Arthur commented that 'St Bride's is grossly overused, whilst there was a 'massive underuse' of the other two buildings, which meant that further building on the St Bride's site, or the use of Ashmount for teaching would not be necessary. The result was a general move away from peripatetic staff to fixed subject classrooms and departmental areas. Clarendon was to house the Nursery and Primary classes to J.5, whilst some secondary departments, notably History and Modern Languages, were relocated from St Bride's to Larchfield, as was Secretarial Studies, previously based at Clarendon. S.1 and S.2 classes also became Larchfield-based. This of course spelt the end of the 'Middle School' concept, which had allowed Larchfield to function with a prep-school age group as it had done before the merger. The M.2 and M.3 classes were renamed Transitus 1 and 2, and Mr Arthur aimed to provide this age-group, who, he stated, always exhibited a 'bouncy, cheerful vitality,' with the '. . . kind of education . . . they need in a changing world'. This did not however prevent a critical article on the subject of lack of consultation about the abolition of the Middle School, written by the Lomond Association Chairman, appearing in the *Association Newspaper*.

However, if the roll in general was falling, boarding numbers were holding up fairly well, with 48 male and 30 female boarders, 56 of whom had homes outside Scotland, (53 outside the United Kingdom altogether). Fifteen of the boys were now housed at Ashmount, and many of the boarders played a part in the undoubted highlight of the School year, 'Rock Nativity', which set both original and traditional songs to modern music.

Elsewhere, Moira Jenkins became Lomond's first graduate with a First Class Honours Degree, (in Astrophysics, from St Andrews); a jazz band was formed by staff and parents; the assessment of Talk and Listening was introduced into the English course from S.1 to S.4, and SCOTVEC (vocational) certification was offered in Computing. The Lomond Society of former pupils also made their first cash award to fund a senior pupil's project for a 'gap year'.

In 1986 Mr Arthur retired after 9 years as Principal. A tribute in the School magazine referred to his 'idealism and passionate concern for education', describing him as 'forward-looking and enlightened' with an 'inexhaustible supply of energy'. He possessed 'infectious enthusiasm', a 'width and depth of educational experience and . . . knowledge of individuals' and was a 'kindly approachable gentleman . . . a good listener'.

The Principal himself commented:

> When I took over in 1977, St Bride's was a cheerful and hard-working girls' school with somewhat limited horizons, while Larchfield was a noisy, busy boys' school with rather erratic academic standards. Lomond today, I believe, is one of the modern independent schools; it is dynamic in response to change, it is a happy and positive school with very high expectations of its pupils, both in academic and in social terms . . . . I have nothing but pride in having had a hand in its creation.

Mr Arthur also pointed out that in his view:

> Lomond has not yet come to terms with the way in which parents, teachers and Governors can get on with their respective roles without hindrance or interference . . . . Any day-school in Helensburgh must face one . . . major problem: that of parental influence.

(Writing in the *Lomond Association Newspaper*, however, Dr A. Macbeth, presented a conflicting view: '. . . the effectiveness of schooling depends to some extent on parents' active involvement . . . . Education cannot be left to teachers alone'.)

Mr Arthur, meanwhile, had nothing but praise for his staff:

> I have never . . . worked with a harder-working staff or one with such a consistently good standard of teaching . . . . I do not believe that there is another school in the UK, independent or state, with as broad a spectrum of pupil ability, which is yet able to produce academic results as good as ours . . . . I know of no school which genuinely has so much to offer as Lomond.

Also moving on in 1986 was Mr Michael Howard, formerly Headmaster of Larchfield, Head of Lomond's Middle School and also Housemaster at various times of four of the boarding-houses. He was praised for his 'ability to be on the pupils' wavelength', and for his 'wide-ranging, devoted and very varied contribution'.

Mr Arthur's successor was Mr Angus Macdonald, Deputy Principal of George Watson's School in Edinburgh, and a Cambridge graduate. He was 36. On taking up the Headship (the title 'Principal' was dropped), Mr Macdonald stated that his sympathies lay '. . . with the honest grafter who gets close to fulfilling his or her potential'. The new Headmaster also stressed his devotion to the outdoor life: 'The outdoors played a large part in my upbringing . . . contentment lay in accessibility to Scotland's hills and lochs.' His appointment to Lomond provided him with an opportunity in an area '. . . where some of my interests have an ideal outlet'. He added that '. . . sport has always featured prominently in my life . . .'. Certainly, over the years to come, Mr Macdonald was to inject a massive amount of outdoor education into the School's extra-curricular programme, in the form of the Lomond Challenge (a triathlon); the Islands' Peaks Race; the expansion of the Duke of Edinburgh Award Scheme and also of sailing, canoeing and hill-walking.

Elsewhere in the School, there were 90 boarders, and whilst a new extension for the Housemaster's family was built at Burnbrae, and central heating was provided for Lansdowne, Ashmount became the new Headmaster's home.

Additionally in 1986, a dilapidated cottage near Inveraray was leased for use in outdoor projects; 180 pupils were involved in a musical production of *Scrooge* in the West Kirk; there was a memorable production of *Dr Faustus* in St Bride's Hall, produced by Mr Robert Parker, and a 'Fun Night' (indoor fair) raised over £1,000 to finance the new 'Period 9' extra-curricular activities. The teachers' dispute in the state sector severely curtailed sporting fixtures, but helped to attract new pupils; carol-singing raised £330 for Yorkhill Children's Hospital Renal Unit, and an Auction in the

Mr A.D. Macdonald, Headmaster Lomond School, 1986 to present.

Hall raised £800 for Clarendon. J.5 held a mediaeval banquet; the Lomond Society held a golf tournament, and a staff/pupil cricket team played three matches. Also, the first Standard Grade examinations were held; the School Shop moved to Clarendon, and the S.6 Centre was relocated in the Bursar's Offices. Local businessmen were invited to lunch in the School to meet staff and pupils, continuing a pattern established under Mr Arthur, and a School v. Society Debate was held, the curious motion being 'Goldfish Should Be Given Away At Fairs'; (the School proposed the motion and was victorious). Other motions at the School's Debating Society included: 'A Woman's Place is in the Home'; 'There is No God'; 'Cannabis should be Legalised', and 'There Should be no Famine Aid for Third-World Countries'. (All defeated.)

By 1987 the roll had reached 480; Mrs Margaret Murray retired after 25 years as Matron of Burnbrae, and sadly, Miss Frances Orr, who had taught Languages and served as Second Mistress (and as Acting Headmistress in 1976) died. Mrs Lillian Gray, the first President of the Lomond Society, was elected to honorary membership.

An impressive sixty extra-curricular activities were offered during the new 'Period 9', which ran from 3.45 until 4.25 p.m. every school day except Friday, replacing 'Prep.' periods with more enjoyable activities. Although a Junior Debating Society argued that 'The Royal Family Should Be Abolished' and that 'Rear Seat-belts Should Be Compulsory', debating as an extra-curricular activity, (previously offered as an alternative to Prep. at 3.45), was effectively killed off by the wide choice of other activities suddenly made available. However, this did not prevent Alison Harper and Elspeth Brown reaching the final of the

Glasgow Rotary Public Speaking Competition. The School also reached the Scottish Final of the UK Prudential General Knowledge Quiz; the prize-money was used to purchase a shield for a School Inter-House Quiz, which took place annually in the Hall on the last day of the Christmas term with Dr Everett and Mr Slavin as quiz-masters, (and sometimes choir-masters and entertainers) until the format was changed to a whole-school written paper in 1995.

The year also saw the introduction of a two-week block of work-experience for all S.5 pupils after their examinations ended, whilst a Lomond Association dance contributed £800 to the Inveraray cottage development. A staff Assembly Committee organised a programme of speakers, interviews, plays and debates which were held during morning assemblies, and Mr Slavin and Mrs Maclaren, (the School Nurse), won a staff mixed-doubles tennis competition. An S.3 band, 'Maybe Tomorrow' was formed, and the *Lomond Association Newspaper* adopted a much-improved glossy format. In addition, S.6 pupils went to London for several days in June, whilst another 'Fun Night' was held.

Meanwhile, the Headmaster commented that examination results had to be 'placed in context'. He felt that too often:

> . . . education is seen as having merely a practical use, . . . as a species of training . . . reducing knowledge to the assessable. Non-assessable but equally vital elements of education become . . . devalued. An obsession with testing is . . . philosophically barren.

Mr Macdonald added that:

> . . . one of the major challenges of the educationalist is to discover that particular area of success . . . that everyone is capable of achieving. . . . An individual's chances of happiness and success . . . depend to a large extent on the self-confidence . . . bred by a sense of personal worth and a sense of achievement.

Consequently, the programme of Period 9 activities was designed to provide '. . . a rich and varied set of stimuli', since, the Headmaster felt:

> . . . the person who has a variety of constructive pursuits is in a healthier and happier position . . . . Who knows what seeds of future happiness are being sown every day in one quiet corner of the School or another? . . . let an individual overcome a challenge, be it physical or mental . . . .

The Headmaster also commented, in an echo of Scandinavian pupil Hanne Halliesen in 1920, on the School's '. . . easy relationships between staff and pupils', based on 'respect, humour, politeness, consideration and concern'. Lomond, Mr Macdonald felt, was 'positive, friendly and caring', and had a 'genuine concern for the individual'.

1988 saw the death of former Headmistress and Governor Miss R. Drever-Smith, during whose tenure of office the School roll had increased by over 30 per cent, whilst a tree was planted at Larchfield in memory of Miss Macmillan who had taught there for 24 years until 1976. In addition, Miss Mary Rawlins retired after a total of 29 years in the Primary Department of both St Bride's and Lomond. The School had waiting-lists for places in several year-groups, and a full-time teacher was appointed to the Nursery to meet increased demand for places.

Meanwhile, fifty per cent of S.6 pupils were studying for 'A' Levels, and a weekly programme of Sixth-Form lectures delivered by guest-speakers was in operation. The Headmaster was also striving to introduce an international element into the Sixth Form.

Elsewhere, the Inveraray cottage was operating, a Careers' Library was set up, an Interhouse Public Speaking Competition was introduced, and J.5 paid a visit to a 'Mediaeval village' in York; (this trip was to become an annual event). The School boasted internationalists in five different sports, and ten pupils and members of staff entered the inaugural Helensburgh 10k. run in May; the School's first Traditional Music Scholar was admitted, the Lomond Society held a London reunion, and a Jordanhill College of Education film crew visited the English Department to film S.4 pupils' solo talks for a Standard Grade demonstration tape.

By this time the School's annual turnover was more than £1,000,000, but major capital expenditure was required, and an Appeal was to be launched the following year. An average increase in staff salaries of 27 per cent over two years led to fee-increases in an effort to maintain the staff/pupil ratio of only 8:1. The Governors stated that: '. . . fee income must meet current expenses and ensure . . . a positive cash-flow . . .'.

By 1989, however, the Headmaster was able to refer to a 'dramatic surge in numbers' and 'an increasing demand for places'. Waiting-lists were growing, and Mr Macdonald felt that the 'physical and educational environment' of the School was 'improving dramatically'. Despite the demand for places, the Headmaster retained a 'commitment to the retention of the human scale . . . and attention to the individual'. To this end, the staff/pupil ratio was, he stated, 'second to none in Scotland'.

Meanwhile, a swelling roll at Clarendon led to the creation of two new classrooms within the existing building, as some year-groups were split into two classes. The Appeal was launched and raised over £150,000, whilst in the evenings the School was used by a variety of community-groups, providing another source of income, including the Franco–Scottish Society, the Civic Society, the Royal Scottish Country Dance Society, and by judo, fencing and Tukido clubs.

In addition, to mark John Logie Baird's Centenary, (1988), an essay competition was run for local schools, and the first prize was won by Lomond's Michele Warren, for her piece on 'The Impact of Television on the Life of a Teenager'.

Elsewhere in the School, the Charities' Committee raised funds for Guide Dogs for the Blind, whilst the School continued its sponsorship of Asian schoolgirl Gemma Rioveros. An Art Exhibition of pupils' work was held in the Studio, the Lomond Association held a 'teach-in' on 'Early Reading', and in the Dining Hall, sales of confectionery, crisps and fizzy drinks were banned, whilst vegetarian options appeared on the menu.

On the sporting front, the Under 13 Boys' tennis team won the Midland Bank Tournament, and Katie Fulton was Scottish Under 16 champion. The hockey team won the West of Scotland championships, and the Headmaster praised the 'huge extra-curricular input' of the staff, whose 'dedication was truly impressive'.

In 1990 the Appeal reached its target of £200,000 and two new Chemistry laboratories were built, whilst one of the existing Biology laboratories was refitted and enlarged. In addition, the remaining grass area at the rear of St Bride's, and a section of the front lawn at Clarendon were tarmacked, and a glass-roofed covered-way was constructed at the rear of St Bride's Hall. The Headmaster commented on the immense goodwill that had been shown towards the School by parents, former pupils and friends, citing as examples the Craft Sale, 'Fayre', and a wine-tasting evening that had collectively raised over £4,000 for the Appeal.

Meanwhile, Michele Warren continued her success, winning the Institute of Physics Prize for the best result in Scotland in the Higher Physics examination; Clarendon held a combined 'Australia Day' and Burns' Night on 26 January, (a regular pattern of visiting Antipodean students to assist at Clarendon had by now been established); three S.5 pupils did their work-experience in Nuremberg; the Traditional Musicians played at the Clan Donald Centre on the Isle of Skye and at Brodick Castle in the first of a series of annual visits, whilst Eilidh Macrae visited the USA with her mother, the Headmaster and Mr Murray, (Deputy Headmaster), and played at the Burns' Society of New York and for the Caledonian Society. Also, the boarders held an 'It's a Knockout' competition, (won by Lansdowne), and the twelfth annual Careers' Convention was held.

In the sporting arena, Kirsty McMeeking won the Over-17 Girls' Discus gold medal in the Scottish Schools' Athletic Championships, and Lomond entered the Island Peaks' Race, involving 200 miles of sailing and 60 miles of hill-running. The School team, composed of pupils, staff and parents, came a very creditable 27th out of 51 (nearly all adult) entries, and obtained sponsorship of £5,000, which was donated to the Appeal Fund.

The recent centenary of John Logie Baird was further marked by the gift from Transitus teacher Mr A. Hope and other individuals connected with Larchfield of an Emilio Coia portrait of the inventor, commissioned by the School. Mr Hope and Mrs C. Malan, (who still teaches Transitus at Lomond), were two of the last-remaining members of staff who had taught at Larchfield when it was a separate entity. The portrait, which was formally presented to the School by Mrs Margaret Baird in 1994, now hangs in the new 'Larchfield Hall', together with a copy of one of Baird's far from illustrious Larchfield school reports, and the War Memorial to the Larchfield dead of World War One. Lomond pupils also visited a Baird exhibition in Glasgow, which included an early television set owned by the School, made in Rhu in 1928 to Baird's design.

Elsewhere, the Headmaster confirmed the School's commitment to helping the individual to flourish and to develop his or her skills to the full, pointing out, however, that '. . . initiative . . . commitment . . . and determination . . .' were required on the part of pupils if they were to achieve maximum benefit. Mr Macdonald also reiterated the 'value of the human element' in a world increasingly dominated by technology: 'If we lose all values, we lose contact with people.'

In 1991 the national 'Year of Sport', the School's involvement in outdoor activities was further extended by the introduction of the Lomond Challenge, a running, canoeing and

Fraser Tyrell and Emma Hassall in the 1991 Lomond Challenge.

cycling Triathlon, which sought to '. . . extend individuals and allow them to discover their own powers', testing entrants' 'sporting versatility, fitness and stamina'. Thirty teams (60 pupils in all) from schools all over Scotland competed for a trophy presented by M.P. John McFall. The Boys' Trophy was won by competitors from Breadalbane Academy, whilst Lomond's Deirdre Galbraith and Elizabeth Fairley won the Girls' award.

Meanwhile, the Lomond Association donated £4,800 for the purchase of a laser-printer, computers and books; it also funded two members of staff (the Headmaster and Mr Dodson) taking Mountain Leadership courses, provided floodlighting for the rear playground at St Bride's and made a donation to the Prize Fund. Additionally it assisted two S.6 pupils to spend a year with Project Trust, teaching in China and South Africa respectively.

The School's traditional contribution to charity was again impressive; T.2B raised £330 for the World Wildlife Fund, helping to purchase four acres in Belize; a Sponsored Swim made £425 for Christian Aid, and the School also raised funds to purchase guide-dogs for the blind. The Housebound Club, (soon to disappear) was still running, and girls from Lansdowne assisted with mentally-handicapped children at the 'Tuesday Club'. There was also another 'It's A Knockout' competition in aid of Comic Relief.

Other notable events included the twelve year-old Jocelyn Wilson's leadership of the British National Youth Orchestra; the appearance of two S.1 pupils on television's 'Fun House', (a test of general knowledge and physical skill), and P.E. teacher Marjorie Coutts' tour of Australia and New Zealand with Great Britain's Women's hockey team. Five pupils also received a Gold Duke of Edinburgh Award, whilst the first of a succession of New Zealand P.E. teachers arrived for a year's stay.

143

Miss J Howie and the Midland Bank U.13 Scottish Tennis Champions, 1992.
Left to right: Jillian Paice, Nicola Middleton, Miss J Howie, Camilla Lamb, Natasha Smith.
(Photo: A. Macdonald.)

Mrs C. Clark with the Transitus Hockey Team (*c.*1981).

Finally, in the year when the 5–14 Development Plan was launched nationally, the Headmaster stated that at Lomond, most pupils got close to fulfilling their potential; '. . . that is the real achievement'.

1992 saw the expansion of the Conservative government's Assisted Places Scheme, which was designed to help children from less well-off families to attend independent schools. Lomond was allocated £125,000, and this sum helped to fund 40 new pupils.

Meanwhile, the Traditional Musicians played in front of an audience of 2,500 in New York's Lincoln Centre, and also appeared on Broadway and on American television and radio. In addition, they collected eight first prizes at the National Mod in Dingwall and at the Glasgow Music Festival.

Elsewhere, Mrs Caroleen Clark, Head of P.E., celebrated 25 years at Lomond and St Bride's; the Under-13 Girls' tennis team were Scottish champions; fifty teams entered the Lomond Challenge, with the School again winning the female section; there were hockey and rugby tours to Eyemouth; the school minibuses clocked up the equivalent mileage of driving to London and back every week; a visiting theatre company staged a presentation on *The American Dream*, and the Lomond Association held a Bridge Evening, Quiz Night and a Ceilidh, raising over £1,000 in the process. The folk-group 'Whistlebinkies' also appeared in concert at the School.

**Miss M. Coutts, left, and Gail Crawford,
Scottish Hockey Captains, 1993.**
(Photo: A. Macdonald.)

In keeping with the Headmaster's belief in the value of outdoor activities, the annual S.6 trip to London was replaced by an 'Outward Bound' leadership and teamwork course, held at Locheil, which was designed to:

> . . . expose pupils to a variety of outdoor experiences . . . to encourage a sense of self-sufficiency . . . and to develop (their) self-confidence by facing up to and overcoming challenges . . . .

In 1993, 92 per cent of S.6 leavers went into some form of higher education, six of them to medical school. The School also had five pupils from Germany studying for a year, and Lansdowne had expanded to twelve dormitories; 47 girls were boarders at some point during the session, the youngest being only eight and a half.

A sign of the times nationally was the talk on drugs given to the Senior school by reformed addict Phil Cooper; weekly

The Traditional Musicians at the Clan Donald Centre, Armadale, 1993.
Back: Claire Campbell, Karen Connor;
Middle: Lynsey Joss, Eilidh McRae, Inga Bewley;
Front: Isla McRae.
(Photo: D. Maxwell.)

careers' lectures delivered by guest speakers also continued, and in the summer, S.5 pupils spent their work-experience fortnight in such diverse locations as France, Germany, the Foreign Office, Majorca, and Derbyshire County Cricket Club. Four senior pupils also went under canvas in Svalbad (Norway) for seven weeks in the summer during a 'Young Explorers' course.

In sport, the number of internationalists had increased to 9, all in different areas; Marjorie Coutts was Captain of the Scottish Ladies' Hockey Team, and pupil Gail Crawford was also Captain of the Scotland Under-18 Team. Ten gold medals were won at the County Sports; football was introduced as a competitive sport by Head of Maths Mr Slavin, and a keep-fit scheme for Clarendon pupils also began. In the Lomond Challenge, the School recorded victories in both the male and female sections, and in the Island Peaks' Race, Nicholas Barclay and Colin Houston broke the youth record for hill-running on Mull. Cricket, which had been reintroduced to the School by Head of English Dr Everett in 1985, reached First Eleven standard, and the School recorded notable victories over Hutchesons' and Morrison's First Elevens before going on tour, playing matches against R.G.S. Newcastle, Barnard Castle School and King's School, Tynemouth. This was the first of four cricket tours that would be held during the next few years.

Other innovations included the introduction of kilts as part of the official School uniform; a three-day conference for S.5 pupils run by the Industrial Society at the Rosslea Hall Hotel; a change of venue for the School Dance, from St Bride's Hall to the Commodore Hotel; an Art Exhibition staged in the Studio by three former pupils, and an appearance on Jimmy Mack's Radio Clyde programme by the Traditional Musicians.

Mrs E. Maclean, right, with former pupil Kirsty Wither at one of the regular FP Art Exhibitions held in the Studio (now the Music Studio) during the 1990s.

147

Meanwhile, Michele Warren recorded a double first at Cambridge; various Lomond Association events raised £3,500 for litter-bins, mini-bus seat-belts, books and prizes, whilst an Evening of Music and Poetry Reading was held in memory of Dr Mark Selwood, former pupil of Larchfield and Lomond, who had been killed whilst climbing in 1990. The Evening marked the publication of a fund-raising anthology entitled *On The Edge of Silence*, the proceeds of which would go to help establish the Mark Selwood Training Centre in Nepal (for Medical and Health Management training).

In 1994, the School was inspected by a team of Her Majesty's Inspectors, and emerged with a glowing report. The Inspectors commented on the School's:

> . . . very healthy prevailing ethos . . . excellent relationships, high morale and evident concern for individual pupils' welfare.

They also praised the '. . . range and quality of extra-curricular activities and the level of staff involvement in them . . .' and the '. . . high standard achieved by the great majority of pupils in their classwork and in external examinations'.

Also in this year, the School won the Rotary Club of Dumbarton's Public Speaking Competition; the Traditional Musicians once again visited the USA; the staff staged a pantomime written by Modern Languages teacher Mrs K. Warden, and the Charities' Committee raised £300 for the Glasgow Children's Hospice. James Reid of S.6 spent an exchange year in Germany, and in a gesture that rekindled the ghosts of wildlife past, the visiting New Zealand P.E. teacher gifted two geese to Burnbrae.

The Headmaster with Anna Semenova, Lomond's first pupil from Russia.
Anna was sponsored by a number of prominent local businessmen. (Photo: D. Kader.)

Mrs Eileen Drummond. (Photo: Miss J. Howie.)

Elsewhere, Mrs Drummond, Assistant Headteacher in charge of Clarendon, and Miss Howie, of the Primary Department both celebrated 25 years at St Bride's and Lomond, and received presentations from the Staff, Governors and Lomond Association. The Association also equipped the Studio as a lecture-theatre, purchased a rescue-boat, and changed its name to *Lomond P.T.A.* in the interests of greater clarity.

Meanwhile, the School entered a team in the Scottish Schools' Equestrian Championships at Gleneagles; the Under-Thirteen Girls' tennis team won the Midland Bank Tournament for the third year running, (the Under-Thirteen Boys' team losing in their final), and on their tour to Lancashire, the Cricket Team recorded a remarkable victory over Arnold School, Blackpool, who a few days earlier had beaten Manchester Grammar School, one of the top cricketing schools in England. The Headmaster referred to this victory as '. . . one of our best-ever team performances'. Jonathan Coates was also capped for Scotland's Under 16 Cricket Team.

In 1995, specialist teaching in Art, Geography and History for T.2 was added to existing French and Science, and Nursery hours were extended. Mr W. Murray retired after thirteen years as Deputy Headmaster, to be replaced by Mr W.G. MacKenzie, previously Assistant Headmaster, and the School welcomed its first pupil from Russia. A School Fair (not 'Fayre' this time), celebrated 150 years of private education in Helensburgh (the assumed date for the origin of Larchfield being 1845, although the present building was not erected until 1858). There was also a concert in the West Kirk in honour of the event, which of course also marked the passage of 100 years since the foundation of Helensburgh High School in Charlotte Street. Interestingly, this year was also the last in which the National Anthem was sung at the annual Prize-Giving. It would be replaced the following year by the School Orchestra's 'Ode to Joy'.

The School's Islands Peaks' Race team, 1995.
The Headmaster is on the extreme left.

149

Elsewhere in the School, the Music Department staged the incredible number of 16 concerts and public performances; the first Lomond Folk-Concert was produced by Head of Computing Mr S. Kilday, and Larchfield Transitus pupils appeared in a superb production of *Oliver* under the direction of Mrs J. Brown and Mrs S. Smith.

In the Island Peaks' Race, Lomond crossed the line first, but were denied victory on a technicality: the Under-Fifteen Girls' tennis team and the Under-Thirteen Boys both won their Midland Bank titles, and the Rugby First Fifteen had its most successful season ever, recording 16 wins out of 22. At this point Lomond had recorded 19 internationalists in 13 different sports.

Meanwhile, a P.T.A. Race Night, replacing the more sedate Bridge Night, raised over £1,000, and in total £3,500 was raised for computer equipment, particularly for the use of Clarendon and Transitus pupils. CD ROM was also introduced to the Library.

On the outdoor front, pupils attended a Duke of Edinburgh residential course which gave instruction in training Mountain-Rescue search-dogs, and S.6 pupils helped to construct paths and steps in Killearn Glen under the guidance of Head of Biology, Mr W. Jennison; they also turned their hand to archaeology, discovering the 'Ladies' Linn', a ruined stone arch over a burn where village women used to wash their clothes.

Interestingly, in view of the enormous programme of extra-curricular activities, ex-Principal David Arthur commented that nearly twenty years after its formation, the School '. . . still offers that extra dimension to education . . .' and referred to the staff's 'enthusiasm, commitment and willingness to go that extra mile . . .', whilst Mr Macdonald added that he had:

> . . . no doubt about the need for independent schools, nor about the support from parents for that need. In fifty years' time, my successor will be saying much the same.

However, in 1996 a falling roll led to staff cuts, (the equivalent of three full-time posts had to be lost), and also to a move towards two-form entry where previously there had been three classes in each year-group. There was in addition a major overhaul of the School's timetable. Instead of eight periods of forty minutes in a day, running from 8.55–3.45, there were to be six fifty-five minute periods, running from 8.30–3.25. This would have the advantage of allowing more light for rugby and hockey-practice in the winter, (a problem first noted in 1921), and also improve road-safety, but in addition, it was felt that the change would provide 'more effective learning units', and would also minimise the time lost by pupils 'commuting' between Larchfield and St Bride's in between lessons. Additionally, the new system would provide daily contact with pupils for teachers of Higher subjects, whilst the introduction of Computing and key-boarding skills for S.1 pupils, and of Modern Studies and Business Studies at Higher helped to provide a more balanced curriculum. Personal and Social Development was also introduced for all secondary pupils, to be delivered by form-teachers in a twenty-five minute 'slot' after registration every Friday. The aim was to teach 'lifeskills, values, self-esteem and individual responsibility'. As the new teaching-day was ten minutes longer than the previous one, (once breaks and lunch-hours were taken into account), the Headmaster was able to say that he had added the equivalent of five and a half more days to the session. Longer mornings were also expected to improve pupils' learning.

Other developments saw the introduction of extra lessons for borderline Higher candidates after school in the second term; Higher Prelim. examinations were moved from early January to the middle of February; at Clarendon a new Music classroom, and also a Technology room were created, whilst the old Music room was turned into a Resource Centre with CD ROM. Learning Support teacher Mrs W. Macdonald was relocated in the old library at Clarendon. In addition, a small Art Gallery was created at Larchfield, whilst the gymnasium and the Art block were reclad.

Meanwhile, despite the award of 23 Academic Ties at the start of the 1995–6 session for six grade 1s or better at Standard Grade, or four grade As and a B or better at Higher, the Headmaster referred to the School's 'diversity of achievement' rather than its concentration on the academic alone. The accuracy of this remark was borne out by an impressive list of pupil achievements, as eight pupils obtained Gold Awards in the Sharp UK Maths Challenge, together with six in the Junior Section; Ben van Well won a Gold Medal in the British Physics Olympiad, placing him in the top 15 entrants in Britain; S.1 History pupils won £1,000 of computing equipment in the Bank of Scotland's 'Money Matters' competition, and were invited to a celebratory lunch at the Bank's headquarters, whilst Maresa Macbeath appeared on Esther Rantzen's 'Children in Need' TV programme as one of the 'five most talented youngsters in the UK'. Later in the year, Maresa also appeared in the National Youth Theatre's production of *Annie*.

Additionally, the Traditional Musicians played at the opening of the new Post Office Building in Edinburgh, and won four medals at the National Mod., whilst a 'Big Band' was also formed and gave its first performance at an Open Evening. Duncan McKerracher was a member of the Scottish Under 20 Triathlon team, Jonathan King represented the Scottish Schools' Golf Association, and the Chess Team reached the final of *The Times* competition. There was a hockey tour to Holland, and a self-defence course was attended by thirty pupils during the February half-term.

Elsewhere, another former pupils' Art Exhibition showed the work of four professional artists, whilst eight years of funding Gemma Rioveros came to an end as she found a post as an Administrative Officer in Manila at the end of her studies; an East African child was to be supported instead.

On the boarding front, there were forty boys in Burnbrae, where Miss Alexander retired as Matron; Lansdowne hosted both the joint Hallowe'en Party and the Barbecue, and winter snowfall provided the conditions for a Burnbrae/Lansdowne snowball fight, in which the girls were unfortunately rather outnumbered!

Meanwhile, the P.T.A. donated £7,000 for IT equipment and £1,000 for refurbishment of the School yacht, and also held a Pet Show at Ardencaple to coincide with the cricket and tennis matches against the Lomond Society in June. Mr R. Kinloch retired after 21 years of service on the Board of Governors, including 14 as Chairman. He was replaced by Mr Sandy Reid, whilst Mrs Caroleen Clark, Head of P.E., and Mrs Eileen Drummond, Assistant Headteacher in charge of the Primary Department, also retired after 29 years' and 27 years' service respectively. Mrs Drummond's replacement was Mrs C. Greig.

The St Bride's site before the fire of 1997.
The various additions and extensions to the original house of 1859 can clearly be seen. The four sections in the foreground of the picture were destroyed in the fire, leaving the Studio (the Music Studio in 2002) on the extreme left, the block to the right of the Studio (A.N. Paterson's Edwardian extension), St Bride's Hall (centre rear) and the lighter-coloured English block, housing the Library

and the Bridesian Library upstairs. On the left of the rear playground are the P.E. changing-rooms and the gymnasium (untouched by the fire), whilst to the right of the playground is the Science block, also untouched. In the foreground, right, is the tennis court laid out in 1928, which is now the site of the new Larchfield Hall.

St Bride's burns in the early hours of 27 February 1997. (Photo: M. Wolfenden.)

The 1997 Fire

On Thursday 27 February 1997, pupils and staff arriving to start the School day found the streets surrounding the School blocked off by police. Through car windows the news was quickly passed around: 'There's been a fire—a bad one.' Just how bad was quickly revealed. Whilst the back of the building had escaped, the main house—the old Ardenlee, dating back to 1859—had been totally gutted. The fire had apparently begun in the small hours of the morning in the Headmaster's office, and had quickly spread to the top floor, raising suspicions that another fire had been set there, as the main staircase was untouched. The flames could be seen from Greenock and Rosneath, and took 6 fire-engines more than three hours to extinguish. (A passing taxi-driver had alerted the fire-brigade at 3.20 a.m.) The Maths and Computing classrooms, the Staffroom and the Sixth-Year Centre were completely gone; in the downstairs rooms unaffected by the fire itself, (Mr Parker's English and Mr Taylor's Geography classrooms, and the offices belonging to the Bursar, Mr MacKenzie, and the secretaries), water from the firemen's hoses had caused much damage to files and pupils' work. Meanwhile, in Mr Macdonald's office, metal filing-cabinets lay twisted totally out of shape by the tremendous heat, and all of the antique furniture presented by the Guild in 1954 in memory of Miss Renton was totally destroyed. The damage was estimated at £2 million.

As fate would have it, the Headmaster and Depute Head were in Germany, visiting Lomond's 'exchange' schools in Leipzig. Senior Master Mr McKellar marshalled shocked staff and pupils in Larchfield dining-hall; sadness, anger and disbelief were the dominant emotions. However, there was no question of pupils being sent home; Head of Maths Mr Slavin quickly drew up a timetable for the whole School, using every available space at Larchfield and Clarendon; the English Department, for example, taught all of its four Higher classes at the same time in the dining-hall; both staff and pupils had to show tolerance and make allowances, and they did so.

The fire-brigade and police were soon discussing the possible causes of the fire; arson was strongly suspected, and certainly the blaze followed a campaign of persistent vandalism during weekends and evenings at both St Bride's and Larchfield. There had also been a blaze causing £50,000 of damage at the Templeton Library, just down the road in John Street, the previous November. No one, however, was ever arrested for the crime, if crime it was.

Messages of support and sympathy flooded in from other schools, including Rhu Primary, which had suffered its own fire in the not-too-distant past, and from parents and former pupils. Current pupils sold home-baking and donated the proceeds to the building of the 'new school'. The phrase was significant, for never for a moment was there any doubt that there *would* be a new school; it was just a question of how long its construction would take. The other question was: how would the School manage in the meantime? In fact, there was, surprisingly, much to be thankful for: Larchfield was unaffected, and as well as containing the Transitus classrooms, the building also housed the School dining-room and kitchens, in addition to several secondary departments. St Bride's East wing was untouched, so the work of the Science and English Departments could proceed

The aftermath.
The Headmaster's, Mr Mackenzie's and the Bursar's offices after the fire, which apparently began in Mr Macdonald's room, (extreme left). (Photo: A. Macdonald.)

St Bride's after the fire.
The lower portion of the blackened section was the Headmaster's study. (Photo: M. Everett.)

St Bride's after the fire.
(Photo: A. Macdonald.)

St Bride's awaiting demolition several months after the fire.
On the right of the picture, the 1946 Jubilee Tree can be seen in flower for the last time.
(Photo: M. Everett.)

unaffected once the ruins of St Bride's that were still standing had been declared safe, (as they were only a week or so after the fire). By great good fortune, St Bride's Hall, designed by A.N. Paterson, was unharmed apart from charring to beams and water-damage; Miss Renton's portrait had been carried to safety by firemen. The oak table and chair, gifted by pupils in 1928, also survived. Paterson's Bridesian Library, with Evelyn Beale's plaque of St Bride, perhaps the spiritual home of the former pupils of St Bride's, (as it began in 1924 as their 'Club Room'), was also untouched, as were the Studio and the Gymnasium. What the School needed were classrooms: three Maths, one Computing, one English and one Geography, and also a staff-room, Sixth-Year Centre and offices. Once planning permission had been obtained, a giant two-storey Portacabin appeared on the rear St Bride's playground during the Easter holidays, whilst a smaller one at the front of the building housed the Headmaster, Deputy Head and secretaries. Not a day's, or even much more than an hour's, teaching had been lost.

All that remained now was to draw up plans for the new building, and to obtain Planning Permission. Since Lomond had a qualified architect in Senior Master and Master of Works, Mr Ian McKellar, he was appointed to design the new Lomond School, with G.D. Lodge and Partners as executive architects. The plans were able to accommodate three floors within the same height as the old St Bride's, (which had had only two floors), because of the great height of the old Victorian ceilings. This in turn allowed for the disposal of the Larchfield building, as all the departments located there could be accommodated in the new school. The only problem was the resiting of the dining-hall and kitchens from Larchfield, but Mr McKellar solved this difficulty by building a new hall (subsequently named the 'Larchfield Hall' in 1999) on the site of the St Bride's tennis-court, which had itself been opened in 1925. (Even earlier, a fountain had occupied the site, when Ardenlee had been built as a private house in 1859.)

Katie Fulton on the St Bride's tennis court, now the site of the new Larchfield Hall, (The Dining Hall).

Before the building could get under way, however, Planning Permission had to be obtained, and the School's neighbours mounted a determined campaign to have the proposals rejected, but after several public hearings and a site-visit by Councillors and protesters, Planning Permission was granted in October. Demolition soon took place, and the foundations of the new school were laid in December.

Perhaps the most notable feature of 1997, however, was the remarkable spirit of all those connected with the School. A staff that had been shocked by news of down-sizing just over a year previously were united in their efforts to ensure that pupils' education, both curricular and extra-curricular, remained undamaged, and pupils never for a moment took advantage of the situation. As Transitus teacher Mrs Catriona Malan wrote in her article in the June 1997 edition of the P.T.A. *Newspaper*:

> Much like a wartime situation, an incredible feeling of comradeship united staff, pupils and parents, to say nothing of former pupils and teachers . . . a time of upset and difficulty quickly roused determination to carry on, bloody but unbowed.

Mrs Malan also expressed this spirit in the last verse of her poem about the fire:

Arson in Academia

No tame beast, this; no pet
That chews hissing rose stalks,
Crunches hedge tinder
Then shimmers the air
With grateful smoky breath.

Nor something domesticated,
Trained to lick clean the brown hills,
Graze on stubble, but obedient
Within the confines
Of the beaters' brooms.

This was a savage thing
Loll-tongued and hungry,
Sent to sniff out skirtings,
Snatch papers, gnaw marble;
No respecter of property

Like a wolf that breaches the henhouse
Leaving the toothmarks of its anger.
But the hens survived.
And the cocks will crow tomorrow
With a Phoenix's voice.

The demolition of St Bride's.
(Photo: A. Macdonald.)

Opposite: **St Bride's in ruins as demolition nears completion.**
(Photos: M. Everett.)

Preparing the foundations for the new building, January 1998. (Photo: A. Macdonald.)

The St Bride's site cleared and the foundations of the new building laid, February 1998.
(Photo: A. Macdonald.)

The skeleton of the new Larchfield Hall, March 1998. (Photo: A. Macdonald.)

Additionally, a pupil, writing of the building that had been lost, commented:

> I remember standing for the first time in the front hallway, amazed that the floor was carpeted, and watching people coming up and down the stairway as if they were in, well, a house . . . there was a sense of history to St Bride's, built up over 140 years, destroyed in a night.

However, after the fire, the same pupil realised that:

> I was wrong to believe that St Bride's felt like a home just because (it) used to be one; it still does, even in a Portacabin . . . one of the teachers reminded us . . . that the School was more than just the buildings, it was primarily the individuals, the community inside . . . . We suffered more than the building did, but maybe our loss made us value more deeply what we have as a School.

The Headmaster, too, commented that: '. . . the quality of human resource at Lomond is a remarkable one', and added that the year had shown '. . . the true value of community spirit'. There was a desire to '. . . create something really worthwhile out of the ashes of the old building . . .' whilst the 'bold' decision to '. . . dispose of Larchfield . . . was not taken lightly'.

That it was 'business as usual' for the rest of 1997 was made clear by the fact that in the summer, Lomond came fourth in Scotland in terms of the number of A/B passes at Higher. In addition, a record 29 academic ties were awarded, and Ben van Well this time won a Gold Medal in the UK Senior Maths Challenge.

Musically, Mr I. Macdonald's Big Band gave its first major public performance at the Victoria Halls, where the Senior and Junior plays were also staged, and where the summer examinations were held too; the Traditional Musicians entertained the International Rotary Club Convention on the *Waverley* and a Lomond Young Singers' Group was formed.

In sport, the Hockey Team toured Holland; Jonathan King represented Scotland at golf; Gillian Murray was the Scottish Under 18 Trampoline Champion, and the Under 13 Girls' Tennis Team yet again won the Midland Bank Championship. Duncan McKerracher represented Scotland Under 21s in the Triathlon; the School was fourth in the Youth Section of the Island Peaks' Race, and a Lomond pair, Andrew Jamieson and Eleanor Black, won the mixed section of the Lomond Challenge. The 1924 Gareloch One boat *Galatea* was gifted to the School by former Governor Mr J. Pollok-Morris, whilst Martin Feeley was Scottish Swimming Champion in his age-group.

Fund-raising, both for the School and for charity, also proceeded normally: the P.T.A. raised over £11,000 in the year; a Non-Uniform Day made £396 for UNICEF; 'Red Nose Day' made £173, and S.1 raised £125 for the 'Blue Peter' Leprosy Appeal, whilst Form 2B restored the sight of seven people in the Third World. An Appeal was also launched to provide 'educational enhancements' for the new building, specifically IT for the twenty-first century.

Elsewhere, there was another F.P. Art Exhibition; the School reached the semi-final of

As Mr Arthur had prophesied: New Lomond pupils from Yinghao School in China outside Glasgow University, 1997. (Photo: A. Macdonald.)

the Bank of Scotland Debating Competition; the Conservatives beat the SNP into second place in a mock election; the P.T.A. held a Ceilidh and a Race Night, whilst a 'Christmas Cake Baking Group' was set up at Lansdowne. A weekly *Newsletter* to parents was also instigated to replace the *Lomond Association Newspaper*, which would cease production the following year.

Meanwhile, a Technology Club was started at Clarendon, and four pupils won a £100 prize in the 'Heatwise Young Technologists' Challenge', a success which would be repeated in 1998. The Nursery itself was refurbished, and, also at Clarendon, activity periods were introduced and extra-curricular activities expanded with the help of S.6 pupils and parents. In the aftermath of the Dunblane tragedy, security also became an issue in the primary school, and measures were taken to ensure that the building was secure at all times.

On the curricular front, Management and Information Studies was introduced at Higher, whilst Computing and Keyboard Skills were offered in S.1.

A School for the New Millennium

1998 was probably an even more exciting year in the life of the School than 1924 had been. Daily, staff, pupils and parents could see the new School growing. An opening was planned for August, and an extra week's summer holiday was granted (although it was deducted from the Easter holidays of 1999 so that no teaching time was lost), in the hope that the building would be ready, but in the event it did not open until October; to the observer, however, progress still seemed to be amazingly quick. The new School provided classrooms for all secondary subjects, plus Transitus One and Two. The new 'Larchfield Hall' served as an assembly and dining-hall, and was linked to the main building by a covered way with cafeteria tables; (hot snacks became available at break). One of the most remarkable features of the new design was perhaps the sudden transition between the new and the old, as a visitor entering through the new reception area had only to step across a corridor, (passing under I. McKellar's atrium) to find him or herself in Paterson's Edwardian St Bride's Hall, which was to continue to stage musical and dramatic productions. (Plans for a gallery to house sound and lighting equipment at the back of the Hall were eventually abandoned.)

The entire building, which boasted stunning views of the Clyde from its upper floors, was to be networked, as too would Clarendon ultimately be. The Library suite would also have a computer room (developed from the 1924 Music practice rooms) for IT research. Security considerations were paramount, and the building was surrounded by a battery of cameras, monitoring all entrances to the School. All doors were automatically time-locked, and entry for staff was by 'swipe-card'.

Meanwhile the School's neighbours mounted another campaign—this time to save Larchfield from demolition. The building had been sold to Cala Homes, who applied for permission to raze it and build five executive homes on the site. (A previous plan had proposed two blocks of 12 flats.) However, 150 local objectors contacted Argyll and Bute Council, and they were joined in this protest by The Scottish Civic Trust, the Architectural Heritage Society for Scotland, Historic Scotland and the local Milligs Conservation Association. Their argument was based on the fact that Larchfield was in a conservation area, (albeit one liberally sprinkled with post-war bungalows), and was linked with a number of famous historical figures, most notably of course, John Logie Baird, whose son added his weight to the protests from Canada. Council Planning officials recommended refusal of the application for demolition, but Cala warned that this would result in the building lying empty for a long period. In addition, according to the new owners, the retention of the building and its conversion into flats would not be viable; in addition, they did not feel that the building was of any 'great architectural merit'. Nor was it a listed building. In truth, the rear of Larchfield, where a hotchpotch of buildings had been added on over the years, was something of an eyesore, whilst the interior was a rabbit-warren of passages and staircases; arguably the only part worth preserving was the facade on Montrose Street. In any case, after the School's move into the new building in October, Larchfield lay empty for the rest of the year, (and indeed for all of 1999). Mrs Catriona Malan again expressed in verse the feelings of many, at the time of the move:

Leaving Larchfield

Here, within these memory-haunted walls,
Shall we stay on as wraiths
(Ghost troubling ghost in layers of time)
When all is gone, leaving
Silence to fall
Like a soft shroud?

Perhaps, in the far attic,
An unearthly washing machine
Will shudder panes, interrupting
A grey matron darning sheets;
Will disturb a mad-haired
Logie Baird from the ideas
He left us, like a curse.

Perhaps in the staffroom a curved line
Of shimmery women on the window-seat
(Birches showing through their gossiping heads)
Will stop at the sound of footsteps,
Loud as a Lambeg drum, and the Irish
Sigh of a broken-bottomed chair;
Will stiffen at shrills of laughter
(Too merry for these shades to bear)
And the old, gold dog Tina
By the dead fire will lift her head
To sniff, where once a Headmaster hung
Long brown photographs; ranks
Of small smiles—only one head turned—
And gowned adults sober as monks.

Perhaps outside, just audible,
Hollow cries of children will be
Punctuated by the knock of
Invisible balls on long-ago willow, where
Cricket nets no longer billow or catch
Hedgehogs that crouch patiently
For morning's rescuing hands.

Perhaps a bar of sunshine
Will light on spectral underwear
(Bachelor purple, womanless turquoise)

166

That once dripped from string over
A bath defaced by stain graffiti;
Will brighten the narrow toilets that
Winnowed the desperate: thin ones in,
Wide ones forced along the passage
Past Room Four that was a dorm
Of open windows, of glacial sheen,
Where children slept like loaves
Stacked in a cold bake-oven.

Then later the woodpecker tap of
Typewriters drilled air
Now filled only with
Faint night-whisperings and, eerie
Through this like a black wisp of sound,
A discourse on Bismarck.

Perhaps beneath the hall's darkbeam arches,
Spectral scents of haddock and curry may
Puzzle the noses of resurrected boys
Treading a shadow stage;
Some in dresses, wigs, stuffed bras, lipstick,
Pretty enough for them to sleep
Wet and uneasy, dreaming about themselves.
Or midnight sounds of cutlery
Will knife through stuffy air, fork over
Auden's measured tones.

Imagine how, down empty corridors,
The banshee whistle of *Winter Wonderland*,
Of *Taking Kathleen Home*, might entertain
A line of hazy apparitions
Pushing towards 'tea and stickies,'
Or fluty trills, ornate as embroidery,
Blown by long-gone breath, might set
Dancing the blue feet of little phantoms
Fumbling claw-handed at rugby laces
On the steaming brim of the plunge-bath.

Will the present haunt the past
As past haunts present: each whispering
To each in the familiar language
Of the teacher and the taught?

> Or will all wise words, shouts, laughter,
> Drifts of song, maths chants
> (Gregorian in melody),
> French talk and violin-notes,
> Seem no more than the swish of trees
> Or the far piping of oystercatchers,
> Long after white dust and
> Silence has fallen
> Like a soft shroud?

October 1998 was a momentous month, as at St Bride's the Portacabins disappeared, and vans full of boxes shuttled between Larchfield and the St Bride's site; desks, chairs and books filled the new classrooms, and pupils and teachers had to learn to find their way around. The experience was almost a surreal one, as, walking along an unfamiliar corridor going who knew where, one suddenly crossed into the 1923 wing and came upon the Library, or the English Department corridor, or found oneself in Paterson's 1909 extension, now the new Music Suite. Larchfield and St Bride's staff, who perhaps had encountered each other only rarely during busy terms, found that they were sharing a staffroom—and a comparatively huge one at that. The School was now truly one unit, and in a surprisingly short time, both staff and pupils made themselves at home. In a third poem, Catriona Malan captured the spirit of the school's rebirth:

The new Lomond School. (Photo: M. Everett.)

168

Lomond Villanelle

Lomond School has risen up anew
Scorning the fire's black mouth, its yellow ire.
Open the doors and let the future through.

From scaffolded ruin the shape of order grew,
Grey blocks began to struggle from the mire,
Lomond School has risen up anew.

Now those who watched its rebirth, those who knew
That though adversity might daunt, it can inspire,
Open the doors and let the future through.

For, proving what so many hold as true—
Burn flesh, burn bones, yet spirit soars entire—
Lomond School has risen up anew.

A metaphor, a guiding point of view,
A text in stone saying: work, resolve, aspire,
Open the doors and let the future through,

Regard with pride the tartan and the blue.
The future, phoenix-winged, flaps from the pyre,
Lomond School has risen up anew,
Open the doors and let the future through.

Meanwhile, amidst all the excitement, the normal life of the School went on; the P.T.A. had now raised £15,000 in total to spend on special projects within the new building; (much of this sum had been raised by the Shop). Sadly, however, the P.T.A. *Newspaper* produced its last edition after a lifespan of twenty years; Mrs S. Hamilton had taken over as Editor after the retirement of Mr D. Fullarton, but a successor to her could not be found, and the advent of the weekly *Newsletter* perhaps suggested that the paper was redundant. In the final edition, the retiring P.T.A. Chairman commented:

> I can think of no other School that encourages the participation of parents as keenly as Lomond . . . (whilst) the support we have had from members of staff has been particularly tremendous.

At Christmas 1998, Mr Bryce Thompson, Janitor for 19 years, and one of Lomond's best-loved characters, also retired. Elsewhere, eight T.1 pupils visited the Royal College of Physicians and Surgeons in Glasgow, (the aim being to familiarise them with hospitals). There was also a rugby tour to Northern Ireland; a second Gareloch, *Circe*, was gifted to the School by Mr and Mrs M. Thornley and a Pipe Band was formed.

Sadly, the new Labour Government stated that the Assisted Places Scheme would be phased out over the next few years and although secondary pupils who held places would be able to retain them for the duration of their time at school, this development indicated that a further drop in the School's roll would be likely over the next few years, unless another source of pupils could be found.

The new building was officially opened on Friday 19 March 1999 by M.P. John McFall at a ceremony in the new 'Larchfield Hall', (the Dining Hall). After his speech, Mr McFall unveiled a commemorative plaque, whilst there were also speeches from Mr A. Reid, Chairman of the Board of Governors, and the Headmaster. Mr Macdonald suggested that faced with the secularisation and individualisation of modern society, 'moral purpose' should be at the heart of education, whilst in an interesting echo of Miss Renton's philosophy, he stated that 'love, truth and beauty' should 'underpin everything that we do', permeating 'the whole ethos of the school community'. After repeating the message of Kurt Hohn, (the founder of Gordonstoun School), that 'we are all better than we know', the Headmaster also extolled the virtue of 'loving thy neighbour', and suggested that '. . . the role of education is to hold a conversation from generation to generation about matters of significance'. Education, Mr Macdonald stated, was not 'about the acquisition of facts. Knowledge is ephemeral but values are what civilise us'. As society becomes 'ever more technically complex', we had a duty 'to make our children more human.' Lomond was 'dedicated' to this aim.

In his own address, the Rev. David Clark, School Chaplain and Minister of the West Kirk, described the day as one of 'celebration and thanks', and paid tribute to '. . . the spirit and sense of community that has enabled this building to develop.' The School, Rev. Clark suggested, 'had . . . a firm foundation rooted in human spirit . . .' upholding 'educational and moral standards'.

Those present, including visitors from the Wilhelm–Lohe School in Germany, were then conducted on a tour of the building, also visiting the new English room (constructed from the former boys' toilets and locker-room in the 1923 East Wing), the new Music room in the Studio and also the one created from the former Geography room, upstairs in A. N. Paterson's Edwardian extension. The Traditional Musicians performed in St Bride's Hall, whilst another focus of interest was the metal Phoenix presented by Lomond's first Headmaster, Mr David Arthur, which stood in the Covered Way outside the Larchfield Hall, symbolising Lomond's rebirth, the spirit of which had been captured by Transitus teacher Mrs C. Malan in her poem. (The Phoenix was later relocated in the entrance foyer.) The official opening was followed by an Open Day, together with F.P. rugby and hockey matches on Sunday, and an Open Evening on Monday.

At the end of the 1998–99 Session, the School roll stood at 415. All rooms in the new building were connected to the Internet, and over 120 computers were now in use. One major innovation was the introduction of 'Successmaker', an integrated learning-system providing diagnostic assessment and individualised interactive learning in literacy and numeracy for pupils with learning difficulties. Meanwhile, the new 'Higher Still' syllabi had been introduced in all subjects with the exception of English and Art, whilst in August

The rear of the original Larchfield after reconstruction. (Photos: M Everett.)

1999, French was introduced into J.5, I.T. and keyboarding into Transitus 2, and Graphic Communication and Core Skills into S.1 The Headmaster commented at Prize-Giving that '. . . the vast majority of pupils are fulfilling their potential in a very positive manner'. To ensure that this continued to be the case, 'Attitudinals', (teachers' A–C grading of pupils' approach to their studies), were issued to parents with much greater frequency, (approximately every six weeks).

Elsewhere, a School Council, on which every Form Class from T.1 to S.6 was represented, was set up to discuss issues concerning pupils; an Amnesty International Group was established; five pupils appeared on Channel Four's 'Fifteen To One' quiz programme; the School yachts *Circe* and *Galatea* (Gareloch Ones) celebrated their 75th birthdays; pupils in the English Department were in e-mail and written contact with children in Russia; the School welcomed its first Artist in Residence, and the new toilet block in the rear playground was opened.

On the charity front, £700 was raised for Children in Need, £405 for UNICEF, £286 for the Nicaraguan Appeal and £242 for Save the Children. (The Headmaster's appearance in a bath of cold baked beans also won a computer from Terry Wogan's radio show for the most original fund-raising idea for Children in Need.)

Numerous individuals also distinguished themselves, with eight F.Ps obtaining First Class degrees, Jennifer Lonnen wining the Institute of Biology's Prize for being the top Higher candidate in Scotland, and 17 Gold Medals being won at the County Sports. Six pupils also achieved the Duke of Edinburgh's Gold Award. F.P. Duncan McKerracher was selected for the British Triathlon team, whilst Sophie Esson was third in the British 405 Championships; Charlotte Dobson was a member of the Scottish and British Optimist Class squads, Kayleigh Harvey won a gold medal at the Scottish Junior Gymnastics Finals, and Antonia Boyce won a gold and silver medal for Gaelic writing and conversation at the Glasgow Mod.

Meanwhile, Chinese pupil Marty Sun featured in Scottish newspapers for achieving three band one A grades at Higher (he was one of only two pupils nationally who did so); Andrew Falconer attended the World Scout Jamboree in Chile and Brazil, whilst S.5 pupils John Hillis and Philippa Robertson travelled to Germany for the opening of the Christliches Gymnasium school.

Later in the year, Cala's revised plans for 25 flats on the Larchfield site were finally approved by councillors in December, by a one-vote margin, after eighteen months of debate and a series of Planning Applications. Eleven flats were to be constructed in the old school building itself, and the other fourteen in a 'Larchfield pastiche' to be erected in the rear playground.

Sadly, 1999 also marked the death of Mary Dutch (Low), who had taught the Transitus age-group for many years before her retirement. Previous Principal, David Arthur, described her as '. . . hardworking, expert in her field, dedicated . . . and prepared to offer real commitment to the School.' Two other long-serving members of staff, Mr W. MacKenzie (Depute Head) and Mrs A. Lyon (Head of Music), celebrated 25 years at St Bride's and Lomond.

In the year 2000, perhaps the major news affecting Lomond concerned a neighbouring

Mrs A. Lyon and Mr W. MacKenzie celebrated 25 years service to Lomond School in 1999.

school; in April it was announced that Keil School, based in Dumbarton since 1925, was to be closed by the Mackinnon MacNeill Trust, which had established the School in the West Highlands in 1915. A decline in boarding numbers and the cessation of the Assisted Places Scheme, in addition to the heavy cost of maintaining the fabric of Helenslee House, (set in 45 acres of ground and formerly the home of the Denny ship-building family), had precipitated the closure. Two hundred and nineteen pupils, (including 45 at Helensburgh's Park Lodge Junior School), 54 of whom were boarders, together with 52 members of staff, (including 33 teachers), had to start afresh elsewhere. By the start of the new session in August 2000, over 40 pupils and several staff had arrived at Lomond, providing a major boost of more than ten per cent to the School's roll.

Meanwhile, as the roll expanded, so did IT use, and at Prize-Giving in June 2000, the Headmaster was able to refer to Lomond's use of the internet, e-mail, an electronic whiteboard and Successmaker, commenting that the School was '. . . in the vanguard of technological use in schools in this country . . .', adding that:

> . . . we will continue to invest significant sums to keep ourselves in the forefront of progress . . . (since) skill-acquisition becomes outdated almost as soon as it is learned.

The Headmaster also pointed out that:

> . . . students can already . . . access information and knowledge that is unknown to a teacher.' This fact '. . . radically challenges the knowledge-based pedagogic model . . . which hasn't significantly altered in generations.

173

Thus:

> . . . we are being driven to consider the first principles upon which education is founded. Students can communicate electronically with . . . other cultures all over the world . . . . What we need is to find the psychological resources to undertake that shift in learning and teaching to which ICT invites us. (It) poses . . . challenges to the way we teach and learn.

However, Mr Macdonald again stressed the importance of traditional human values:

> I believe in measurement and analysis if that means that individual potential can be tracked . . . (But) the greater the focus on quantification, the less the emphasis becomes on those aspects . . . that cannot be measured and which have . . . greater value.

Referring to '. . . Political correctness gone mad, and the stultification of . . . innovation, common-sense and academic freedom . . .' the Headmaster stressed that Lomond would continue to encourage '. . . enterprise and responsibility, teamwork and leadership, courage and determination, care and compassion . . .', stating that:

> . . . we retain our commitment to a broad education, developing character and self-confidence . . . we aim for small class sizes and human scale . . . (Since) the real object of education is to give children resources that will endure as long as life endures, habits that time will ameliorate, not destroy, occupations that will render sickness tolerable, solitude pleasant, age venerable, life more dignified and death less terrible.

Perhaps, a hundred years back in time, Miss Renton might have nodded in agreement.

Other notable events in 2000 included the retirement of English teacher and drama-producer Mr Robert Parker after 21 years' service, and also that of Librarian and R.E. teacher Mrs Anne Bernard after 22 years. Burnbrae also said goodbye to Mrs Boyle after 13 years as Assistant Matron.

Meanwhile, the Traditional Musicians played at the Clan Donald Centre at Armadale on their Skye Tour, whilst pipers Susan Tully and Martin McLellan appeared at the Royal Concert Hall to celebrate 175 years of the RNLI. Amanda Forbes and Eilidh Reid-Foster also featured on TV's 'Children in Need', playing the clarsach in a nation-wide Beatles' medley.

On the charities' front, £164 was donated to the Cancer Research Campaign For Scotland; a Non-Uniform Day produced £200; a sponsored canoe-trip on Loch Lomond produced a similar sum for Amnesty International, whilst the July Canoe Expedition on the Harricanaw River in Quebec, Canada, involving 16 pupils and 3 staff and led by the Headmaster, raised over £5,000.

The PTA also staged a number of events, including a car boot sale, a ceilidh, a quiz-night and a wine-tasting evening, and donated £12,500 to the School for landscaping the south and east sides of the building; (a similar sum had been gifted in 1999 for landscaping at Clarendon). Elsewhere, former pupil Miranda Gill received a first-class Honours Degree in Modern Languages from Oxford; Rosamund Spinnler achieved a Gold Award in the UK Senior Maths' Challenge, whilst there were also five Golds in the Junior Challenge. In addition, on the sporting front, the playing-fields at Ardencaple were drained and resurfaced, whilst Oliver van Well won three gold medals at the County Sports, also winning the Hudson Memorial Trophy.

The Young Enterprise Group were also busy producing Millennium mugs and were able to pay shareholders a 20 per cent dividend; the Geography quiz-team reached the National Finals at Perth, and a party from Lomond joined pupils from Hutchesons' Grammar School and The Glasgow Academy for a trip to California in July.

At Clarendon there were trips to Inchmurrin, Balloch Country Park, Vikingar at Largs, the Hunterian Museum (where J.3 dressed up as ancient Egyptians), and York, whilst Transitus pupils went on a camp to Meigle.

Unfortunately however, a major cloud was cast over the year by the well-documented shambles at the newly-formed Scottish Qualifications Authority (SQA), which resulted in candidates nation-wide receiving certificates for examinations they had not taken (and not receiving certificates for those that they had), and which as a result called into question the accuracy of everyone's grades. Mr Macdonald referred to a 'considerable loss of confidence' in the SQA. However, virtually all of Lomond's candidates received the grades that had been predicted for them, and at the start of the 2000–2001 session, the Headmaster was able to present 20 Academic Ties for six grade ones or better at Standard Grade—a new record. He gave the warning, however, that such success might only serve to heighten pupils' and parents' 'sense of expectation' for similar success at Higher, which would not automatically follow.

The School's own works' team was also busy, as Mr Jennison's Biology laboratory and Dr Everett's English classroom were upgraded, to 'effectively complete the total modernisation of the St Bride's site', as the Headmaster stated. The Library (the 1924 Art Studio) was also converted to a classroom for Transitus pupils, leaving the former 'Bridesian' Library, which had previously been for the use of S.6 pupils only, as the sole library in the School. Meanwhile, the space next to the former library, once the site of music practice-rooms, then of the offices of the Deputy Headmaster and Senior Master, and latterly of a computer-room and careers' room, was also turned into a classroom for English and R.E., whilst an additional computer room was created at Lansdowne. At St Bride's, computers for pupils' research were relocated outside the Maths Department classrooms.

As 2001 began, plans were being made to sell Lansdowne Park and to demolish Burnbrae in order to build a new boarding-house for both boys and girls on the Burnbrae site. Since the closure of Keil School the previous year, Lomond had become the only boarding-school in the west of Scotland, and this position was to be consolidated by the provision of modern boarding facilities. As Planning Permission was sought at the start of the year, it was hoped that the new house could be opened in August 2002. However, experience gained during the process of rebuilding St Bride's suggested that matters might

After 80 years in the School's possession, Lansdowne Park is to be sold in 2003.

not proceed so smoothly, as the Headmaster remarked in a *Newsletter* of January 2001; the new house would bring the School's:

> . . . boarding provision into line with the quality of amenities elsewhere, but I am sanguine enough to know that no progress or development in Helensburgh can proceed without controversy, nor can one guarantee that plans come to fruition . . . .

Meanwhile, in April 2001, Sister Mary Frideswide died at St Mary's Convent, Wantage. As Miss Hensman, she had been Headmistress of St Bride's from 1943–1953, leaving to enter a convent. The year also saw the retirement of Miss Jean Howie, a teacher in the Primary Department at St Bride's and Lomond for 32 years; Miss Howie had devoted an enormous amount of time to girls' hockey and tennis teams during her teaching career. Mrs Elizabeth Maclean, Head of the Art Department, also retired after 16 years' service, and a Dinner was held for both ladies at the Rosslea Hall Hotel.

Elsewhere in the School, the prefect system was altered to allow the entire sixth year to become prefects; interactive electronic whiteboards were installed in the Geography and Graphic Communication Departments, and, also in the library at Clarendon. The boarding-houses underwent a Welfare Inspection by HMIs; three pupils achieved Oxbridge places; a computer room was created at Lansdowne; Clarendon classrooms and toilets were upgraded, and the two Physics laboratories, little changed since their creation in 1964, were refurbished.

Further afield, it was announced that the last of the west end of Glasgow's three girls' schools, Laurel Park, was to merge with Hutchesons' Grammar School on the south side of the city. Laurel Park was itself the product of a 1996 merger between the first of the

Girls' School Company's schools, The Park, (established in 1880), and Laurel Bank School. Since the other west-end girls' school, Westbourne, had merged with The Glasgow Academy in 1991, no single-sex education for girls was now available north of the river. These developments, coupled with the recent closure of Keil School and the apparent imminent threat to Rannoch School in Perthshire, indicated the precarious nature of the existence of small independent schools; however, at Lomond, the influx of pupils from Keil, coupled with many others whose parents had been attracted by the new buildings and facilities, saw the roll increase to 485, an increase of more than 100, or 25 per cent, since the previous year. A number of new staff were consequently recruited.

The year was also notable, as usual, for a variety of pupil achievements; German pupil Irene Spangenberg won an eight-day trip to Paris as one of the top-three prize-winners in an essay competition organised by Alliance Francaise; Transitus pupils won the Final of the Heatwise Technology Challenge; Oliver Gourd played in the National Children's Orchestra; Janie McCathie, Jemma Wurker and Katie Reynolds won the Dumbarton Rotary 'Youth Speaks' competition; (later in the year Janie was also to appear on national television, winning £16,000 on 'Who Wants to Be a Millionaire'), and Charlotte Dobson and Sophie Esson represented Scotland at sailing in the Ladies' section of the Nations' Cup. Charlotte also won the Optimist section of the Volvo Scottish Youth Championships, came fourth in the UK Championships and won the Bronze medal and the Silver Team Medal in the Laser Radial World Championships in Barcelona, whilst Sophie was second in the youth section of the UK 420 National Championships at Weymouth. Meanwhile, Andrew Greer was a member of the British Volvo Under-14 420 Development Squad, and Lomond finished second in the Optimist Class of the Scottish Schools' Sailing Championships.

Elsewhere on the sporting front, Calum Simmister (shinty), Oliver van Well (athletics) and Frazer Bone (golf) received international caps, (Frazer also coming second in the Under-16 Scottish Open). The School also entered the inaugural Scottish Schools Showjumping Championships; S.1 pupils Nicola Ferguson and Fiona Milton, together with Eliza Ritchie of T.1, came first. Unfortunately, however, the Foot and Mouth outbreak led to the cancellation of the Islands' Peak Race, and also severely affected the School's Duke of Edinburgh Awards programme, the Silver Expedition having to be postponed due to restricted access to the hills. The hockey tour to Holland and the visit of a Northern Ireland rugby team had to be cancelled for the same reason. However, restrictions had been lifted in time for Stephen Button and Jonathan Henderson to win the Boys' Section of the Lomond Challenge, and for Alexandra Allum-Smith and Emma Swinnerton to make it a Lomond double by winning the Girls' Section.

Charity work proceeded as usual, however, with over £3,000 being raised during the session. The Junior Amnesty Group collected £260 for the Indian Earthquake Appeal, filled 72 shoe-boxes for children in eastern Europe and also sent letters to a number of Heads of State concerning the abuse of human rights. James Spy raised £193 cycling for Christian Aid, and Gilbert Beveridge also cycled from Glasgow to Edinburgh for Barnardo's 'Children First', whilst a 'Silly Tie Day' raised £145 to aid research into genetic disorders; at the end of the year, clothing and tins were collected for the Glasgow homeless, and foreign currency for Age Concern.

In his Prize-giving speech of June 2001, the Headmaster referred to the planned demolition of Burnbrae: the 'myriad feasibility studies, consultation exercises, adaptations, discussions and planning procedures' had been 'frustrating in the extreme'. The School's objectives were to 'provide a flexible, modern, well-equipped boarding-house suitable for the twenty-first century.' Boarding had '. . . strategic and educational value to the school and the local economy . . . .' The HMIs had given '. . . warm and genuine endorsements for the quality of our boarding set-up . . .' and had been 'impressed by our knowledge of all the students and the detail of our monitoring systems . . .', the aim of which was to '. . . ensure that every individual . . . is encouraged to fulfil their potential as academics and human beings'.

The School's monitoring fell into three categories: academic potential was measured by Cognitive Ability Tests; application by Attitudinals; and involvement by extra-curricular participation. Lomond was 'blazing the trail in education in this country' in the area of individual monitoring to maximise potential.

The Headmaster also referred to the 'huge responsibilities and risks' for staff involved in expeditions and trips. The current climate increasingly sought to 'regulate, protect and cocoon youngsters from the excitement . . . presented by the real world.' Lomond, Mr Macdonald stated, would 'refuse to wrap individuals in cotton wool . . . .'

Another area of interest amongst parents was the new prefect system, which had abolished selection. The Headmaster stated that he was seeking:

to give meaningful responsibility . . . to develop responsible citizenship . . . . To encourage initiative, develop leadership and teamwork skills and engender a sense of worth and self-esteem . . . not for the chosen few alone but for everyone . . . .

Mr Macdonald also referred to the SQA debacle of 2000, commenting that '. . . there are pupils . . . whose faith in what was previously the benchmark and hallmark of Scottish education—Highers—is forever shattered . . .'. The Headmaster also remarked on the 'ever-increasing quantity and levels of assessment . . .' and on 'how important it is . . . that all sectors of the education profession are properly valued and remunerated'. He questioned the assumption that education should be equated with 'The future economic prosperity of the country . . .' as this was, in his view, '. . . a narrowly pragmatic and dogmatic approach . . .' as 'ultimately, the ability to think for oneself is a major raison d'etre for the educational process . . .' this process '. . . may yet produce the changes to society required if injustice and inequality are to be tackled on a global scale.'

By August 2001, the School roll had risen to 500, with waiting-lists in most primary age-groups. The Headmaster commented that '. . . to all intents and purposes we are at capacity.' Fortunately, he was also able to comment that 'faith in the SQA has been restored, as the shambles of 2000 did not recur. Twenty Academic Ties were awarded for six grade ones or more at Standard Grade, and Lomond once again achieved highly impressive pass-rates at all levels, particularly for a non-selective school: Standard Grade 96 per cent pass (83 per cent Credit); Higher 91 per cent pass (75 per cent A or B); 'A' Level 95 per cent pass.

Planning Permission for the demolition of Burnbrae and for the construction of a co-educational boarding-house on the site was eventually obtained in September; at this stage it was hoped that work could commence in January 2002, although this was again to prove premature. Talks were also underway with Argyll and Bute Council to secure a lease on the former Outdoor Centre at Arrochar, which had lain empty for two years; considerable investment would be required by the School to bring the Centre up to standard, however.

The tragic events in America on 11 September were marked by two minutes' silence the following day, and by a special assembly on Monday 17 September at which 'Flowers of the Forest' was played by Pipe Major Susan Tully, of S.6. In that week's *Newsletter*, the Headmaster commented that in the face of such an enormous disaster, the School '. . . could but carry on operating as normally and positively as possible'.

The new session saw the introduction of a Merit system for pupils in S.4–S.6, Bronze Awards being given to pupils who represented the School regularly and reliably in any capacity; Silver to pupils who showed initiative or distinction in one area, or who had gained three Bronze nominations, whilst Gold Awards were reserved for S.6 pupils who had sustained their distinctive input and who had shown a real commitment to their studies, proving good role-models for younger pupils in the School. The School captain, Lindsay Robertson, was the first recipient of the Gold Award.

The P.T.A. continued to thrive, raising £150 by staging a 'Happy Gang' musical performance in St Bride's Hall that was attended by over 200 parents and children, and a further £832 at a Race Night in October. Clarendon staff were busy fund-raising too, collecting £54 from a pumpkin raffle in October, and raising £362 from a Book Fair in November.

As 2001 drew to a close, events included a highly successful production of *Joseph and the Amazing Technicolor Dreamcoat* staged by Transitus and S.1 pupils, produced by Mrs A. Holliman, all nights of which were sold out. The Headmaster described the performance as 'one of the most successful productions in recent years'. Elsewhere, there was a talk for parents entitled 'Scotland Against Drugs', and a 'Languages For Life' forum, in which twelve guest-speakers spoke to pupils on the importance of foreign languages in their lives. In illustration of this theme, the Headmaster and Depute Mr Mackenzie visited Germany in November for the centenary celebrations of the Wilhelm–Lohe School, which had been sending pupils to Lomond since 1977, whilst a survey of recent former pupils found residents in Japan, Hungary, New Guinea, Germany, Guyana, China and Hong Kong; Patrick Hamilton, (significantly after the disaster of 11 September), was working in Jalabad as a translator.

The year 2002 marked the centenary of the opening of St Bride's School on the present site, and also twenty-five years of the existence of Lomond School. Staff numbers continued to grow, with three New Zealand P.E. assistants joining the two Australian and one German 'Gap-year' helpers at Clarendon. The session also saw the employment of an Information Technology Support and Development Officer. Again the Headmaster commented that the School was '. . . exceptionally well-resourced in this area . . .', adding that he '. . . tried to ensure that . . . technology serves our aims as educators.' Ironically, perhaps, a sign of the times was the Headmaster's warning to parents in January that some primary-age pupils were:

> ... using the internet in the early hours of the morning, (making) quite unsuitable contact with other, sometimes adult, users, and posting inappropriate material on other pupils' message-boards.

As part of a programme of classroom-monitoring, cameras were also installed in three classrooms.

At half-term in February 2002, Burnbrae, home to St Bride's and Lomond boarders since 1918, was finally vacated, the residents transferring not to the Arrochar Outdoor Centre as had been planned, but to the former Ardgartan Youth Hostel, also at Arrochar. The Headmaster commented on the Hostel's 'spectacular site', and stated that the boys would '... greatly enjoy the superb location' on the lochside. To help to transport the boys, the School's complement of mini-buses was increased to four, including two new vehicles.

Other events at the start of the year included a non-uniform day in February to raise funds for children in Brazil and Bangladesh, whilst timetable changes saw the schedule for Mondays become the same as that for Fridays, with period one commencing at 8.55 am to allow twenty minutes rather than ten after registration for Assembly. Interestingly, hymn-singing at Assembly was dropped, probably after more than a hundred years, due to the unenthusiastic response of most pupils; this subject had occupied a good deal of time at Heads of Departments' meetings and at those of an especially-formed Assembly Committee before the decision was reluctantly taken.

The former Ardgarten Youth Hostel, home for the boy boarders, February 2002–Summer 2003. (Photo: A. Macdonald.)

Meanwhile, Alasdair Dunlop of T.1 led out the Scotland rugby team at Murrayfield in their match against England; Angus McInroy won a gold medal in the Under-16 shot-putt at the Scottish Schools' Indoor Athletics Championships and a bronze in the Under 17 shot; there was an outbreak of headlice at Clarendon, and a World Challenge Expedition to Bolivia led by Mr Jennison and Mr Carter was planned for summer 2003.

In the spring, Frazer Bone was selected for the Scottish Boys' under 16 golf team, and James Spy and Erin Maconochie reached the UK National Finals in the Dengie Winter League Show Jumping, whilst an S.2 and an S.4 class completed a Scottish Executive questionnaire on adolescent lifestyle.

A feature of the session was the remarkable success achieved in Public Speaking competitions by the S.3 trio of Laura King, Charlotte Stoney and Georgina Wardrop. The girls won the Dumbarton Rotary Competition, came second in the Rotary National Final and also reached the English Speaking Union National Final in Edinburgh; in all these competitions they were usually competing against pupils several years older.

Other notable events in the Spring term included Ben White's involvement in the National Boys' Choir of Scotland, and the inclusion of a number of S.1 pupils' poems in the published Zodiac Anthology.

At Easter, the Headmaster commented in a parents' *Newsletter* that the 'floating' dates of Easter itself were 'an anachronistic frustration that makes little educational sense'. The management were '. . . trying to establish a more rational pattern to the school year'.

Spring progressed into a soggy summer in which a remarkable nine First Eleven cricket matches were cancelled, including the annual fixture against the Lomond Society. Senior pupils completed a school questionnaire on topics including the curriculum, pastoral care, vocational guidance, sport and uniform; Morgan Gladden of T.2 competed in the British Junior Karate Championships in Blackpool, and Mrs C. McElhill's superb production of *Return to the Forbidden Planet* was staged in St Bride's Hall. Visiting Australian pupils from All Saints School, Bathurst, staged a Big Band concert with Lomond pupils, whilst Charlotte Dobson took part in the National Laser Youth Championships, and her younger sister, Anna, participated in Optimist World and European selection trials. Meanwhile, former pupil, Major Phil Ashby, a holder of the Queen's Gallantry Medal, published a book titled *Unscathed*, recounting his exploits with the Marines in Sierra Leone.

In another *Newsletter*, the Headmaster warned that:

> Demand for places at Lomond is such that there are currently parents who wish to place their children here who are having to face disappointment. Virtually all of the primary year-groups are full for next session as are . . . T.2 and S.1 . . . . Parents should not take for granted that there will be places available in August 2003 . . . prospective boarders are also being turned away . . . the new facility will open at the turn of the year with a full house . . . . (However) . . . the scale of the School and class sizes will be maintained at their present level.

Commenting on the curriculum, Mr Macdonald informed parents that Intermediate II had replaced Standard Grade in Information Systems (Computing), Graphic

Communication and Modern Languages. The following session, Art and Business Studies would follow suit, although the decision whether to make the change would be left to the individual departments.

As the summer term proceeded on its depressingly damp course, Nursery pupils took part in a sponsored 'Pedal Push' for Childline; five gold awards were won in the UK Junior Maths Challenge; the Traditional Musicians toured Plockton and Skye, and Charlotte Dobson was selected for the British Laser Radial Team for the European and World Youth Championships in Austria and Canada respectively, winning a gold team medal and silver individual in Canada. Meanwhile, Morgan Gladden was first overall in the Scottish Gymnastics, Vault, Beam and Floor competition, and a musical 'Practice-a-Thon' raised £177.50 for Sargent Cancer Care for children.

The end of term saw the retirement of Mrs Carol Reid, who had taught Physics at the School for 22 years, much of this time as Head of Department, whilst staff, pupils and former pupils were shocked by the sudden death of Eilidh Reid-Foster, a talented musician, at only 18. (Eilidh's death was sadly followed during the summer holidays by that of the Rev. Andrew Mitchell, the School's R.E. teacher since August 2000, at the age of 67, and by that of Miss Carrie Alexander, former Matron at Burnbrae, in October.)

In his speech at Prize-giving speech in the West Kirk, June 2002, the Headmaster referred to the 'talent, energy and commitment of the teaching staff' which was reflected 'throughout the range of extra-curricular activities that are such a key component of the education that we offer.'

> You don't have to theorise or pontificate about it—you can feel it and sense it and know when education is taking place.

Mr Macdonald also touched once again on the '. . . increasingly litigious nature of society and the dangers that imposes,' particularly in regard to the trips, expeditions and visits that form such an important part of Lomond's extra-curricular provision, and he went on to question the need for twice-yearly Care Commission inspections of boarding pupils' welfare.

However, the main thrust of the speech concerned the events of 11 September in New York which had cast a 'pall of insecurity over all our lives' and brought a 'fragility to world peace.' Quoting John F. Kennedy, President of the USA in the early 1960s, Mr Macdonald suggested that rather than stating what they would prefer the world to be like, individuals should ask what they could do for the world, as:

> . . . meaningful change is a bottom-up process . . . change (is) a personal responsibility
> . . . . Keep improving yourself . . . and the area that you occupy at any given time.

Education was important, the Headmaster stated, as it provided:

> . . . enlightenment against the darkness of propaganda and hatred. It promotes tolerance against intolerance . . . and at its best can ennoble the mind and spirit . . .

producing lasting peace in the world.

He added that in his view, '. . . teaching is a noble profession' as it '. . . enriches lives . . . and aids understanding of other cultures.' Whilst '. . . wings can be singed if we fly too close to the sun . . . that is preferable to not flying at all.'

In a year that would see in August the 25th Anniversary of the opening of Lomond School, and the centenary of the opening of St Bride's, the conclusion of the Headmaster's speech, with which Miss Renton would have wholeheartedly concurred, also make a fitting conclusion to this book, as it sums up the spirit and ethos that has infused this small independent school on the Clyde estuary for the last hundred years:

> I have faith in the talents and abilities of the pupils . . . I believe that our international element, our ethos and our teaching help to develop tolerance and understanding which . . . can make a difference in the world . . . . We can all improve ourselves and affect others around us, and that process can turn back the tide of intolerance . . . and . . . produce . . . justice . . . . What we do can make a difference . . . . Some of us are gardeners (sowing the seeds and doing the spadework); others are sculptors (shaping future lives) or alpine gardeners (encouraging pupils to heights they only dream of). All count.

Postscript

The story of Helensburgh High School, St Bride's, Larchfield and Lomond Schools has been one of endurance and adaptation that spans three centuries. That this has been the case is due to the vision of those who have served as the Directors of the Girls' School Company, as Directors and Governors of the four Schools, and as Headteachers and members of the Schools' management-teams. This vision led to the establishment of the Girls' School Company in 1879; to that of the Company's first school, The Park School, in 1880, and to the founding of Helensburgh High School in 1895. In the twentieth century it prompted the move to the Ardenlee site, (renamed St Bride's), in 1902; the merger of St Bride's with Larchfield in 1977, and the design and construction of a School for the twenty-first Century after the 1997 fire. The quality of endurance, meanwhile, enabled the Schools to survive two World Wars; periods of falling rolls; the abolition of the Direct Grant and Assisted Places Schemes; runaway inflation during the 1970s that prompted large pay-rises for staff; actual and proposed mergers and, once again, the devastating fire of 1997.

It might be thought that there is little in common between the new Lomond School of 2003, and the tiny Helensburgh High School of 45 pupils that opened in Kinnear House, Charlotte Street, in 1895, or between today's Lomond and the expanding St Bride's School, which opened on the present site in 1902, almost exactly one hundred years ago. Certainly, the school buildings are different (although parts of the old St Bride's remain); customs and behaviour in society in general are different; the opportunities available to young people, especially girls, have radically altered as the previous few pages of this book have shown. (It was in an attempt to bring this about that Helensburgh High School was founded.) Helensburgh itself has also grown tremendously in size, but surprisingly perhaps, the ethos of the School seems to have remained largely unchanged. If this is indeed the case, it must in the main be due to the philosophy of those who have led the three schools over more than a century; in fact, the values and attitude to education of the School's first and longest-serving Headteacher, Miss J.B.M. Renton, seem to have been remarkably similar to those of the present Head, Mr Angus Macdonald. To both, the importance of offering young people as many opportunities to 'do something . . . rather than do nothing' (Miss Renton) and so to maximise individual potential has been paramount, as these pages have shown. In addition, small classes, a constant over 108 years, have helped staff to provide individual attention for the pupils in their care, whilst the relatively small size of the School itself (the roll has never exceeded 600, including the Primary section), has fostered the excellent teacher-pupil relationships that were commented on by the Scandinavian pupil, Hanne Halliesen in 1920. Meanwhile, Hanne's presence at St Bride's and Miss Renton's exhortations to her charges to learn German immediately after the end of World War One in 1918 are evidence that she shared Mr Macdonald's view of the importance of an international dimension to the School, both to provide opportunities to young people from overseas, and to counteract any tendency to insularity.

All these positive qualities of the School, plus numerous others, have meant that the thousands of pupils and hundreds of teachers who have studied and taught at the four schools have been fortunate in their experience, and as we begin a new millennium, the hope is that Lomond will, over the next century, continue to provide a tremendous range of opportunities of all kinds for those who attend it. Certainly, all the omens for the continued success of the School are positive: it possesses a new building, incorporating the best of the old in the Bridesian Library and St Bride's Hall, both of which would be instantly recognised by Miss Renton; a new co-educational boarding-house that opened in April 2003 under the leadership of Head of Boarding Mr A. Minnis and Mr and Mrs Macdonald, Houseparents, has been constructed on the site of the old Burnbrae, and will confirm Lomond's place as the only boarding-school in the west of Scotland; the School roll is over 520, up 140 on three years ago; there are plans for a new games' hall and enhanced sports' facilities; Higher and Standard Grade pass-rates were over 90 per cent in 2001, and an inspection early in 2003 hopefully confirmed the School as a member of the prestigious Headmasters' Conference Group of Schools (HMC).

Thus the School has developed and expanded far beyond the dreams of its founders, the gentlemen of the Girls' School Company, in 1895, and there is no reason to doubt that whatever the challenges and changes ahead, locally, nationally and internationally, it will continue to enhance the lives of the young people fortunate enough to attend it in the years to come.

Prospiciamus (Let us look forward).

Dr Martin Everett
April 2003

The new boarding-house, February 2003. (Photo: A. Macdonald.)

The rear of the new Burnbrae which opened in April 2003. (Photo: M. Everett.)

Bibliography

From the Alleghenies to the Hebrides, Margaret Fay Shaw, (Canongate Press, 1994)

Variety without Disorder. A History of St Columba's School, 1897–1997. Dr Susan Milligan, St Columba's School, 1998.

Bridesian Magazines, 1911–1969; 1971. *Alpha* 1977–1981. *Lomond Annals* 1982–2000.

Lomond Association Newspapers.

Helensburgh Directories, various years (Macneur & Bryden).

The Private Schools of Helensburgh—An Outline History up to World War Two. (Lomond School Neighbours' Group, February 1998).

The Helensburgh and Gareloch Times 1895–1910.

The Helensburgh Advertiser 1970–1976.

The Bridesian Guild Magazines 1969–1975.

Illustrated Architectural Guide to the North Clyde Estuary. F.N. Walker with F. Sinclair, (Royal Incorporation of Architects in Scotland, 1992).

Helensburgh in Old Picture Postcards, P. Drayton. European Library, 1985.

Around Helensburgh. K.N. Crawford and A. Roberts, Tempus Publishing 1999.

Miss Renton.

Miss M.C. Bell.

Miss M.N. Hensman.

Miss R.D. Smith.

Miss C. Campbell.

Mr D. Arthur.

Mr A.D. Macdonald.

Headteachers of Helensburgh High School, St Bride's and Lomond Schools, 1895–2003

1895–1929	Miss J.B.M. Renton	(34 years)
1929–1943	Miss M.C. Bell	(14 years)
1943–1953	Miss M.N. Hensman	(10 years)
1953–1972	Miss R. Drever-Smith	(19 years)
1972–1976	Miss C. Campbell	(4 years)
(1976)	Miss F. Orr (Acting Headteacher)	
1977–1986	Mr D.S.C. Arthur	(9 years)
1986–	Mr A.D. Macdonald	(17 years to 2003)

Acknowledgements

The author would like to thank the following people:

The secretarial staff of Lomond School, in particular Mrs E. Wylie and the late Mrs Irene Giles for their help in typing and correcting the manuscript.

Mr W. Anderson, of Kenilworth Road, Bridge of Allan, for kindly making available his collection of family photographs and other items connected with St Bride's and Larchfield.

Mrs Isabel Clark, of Lennox House, Edinburgh, for her information and reminiscences concerning St Bride's during and after World War One.

Mr D. Arthur for kindly lending photographs and other material.

Mrs C. Malan for permission to reproduce her three poems.

Mrs E. Maclean for her photographs of buildings connected with the School.

Mr M. Wolfenden for permission to use the photograph on p.154.

Miss J. Howie for kindly proof-reading the manuscript.

Every effort has been made to attribute photographs correctly to their photographers. The author apologises for any inadvertent errors or omissions

List of illustrations

Index